Tenaciously Teaching Teenagers

The most rewarding aspect of being a teacher isn't how you get through the content, but how you reach your students and have a lifelong impact. In this funny and heartwarming book, Pamela Jean Matusz lets us into her classroom and shows how she connects with an often-hard-to-understand species—teenagers!

She provides stories and strategies on earning respect, using humor, and being your weird self, giving students a voice, earning respect, and making yourself human. She also demonstrates how to put students into the lesson, grade what you say you're grading, teach and not penalize, address bullying, and understand where parents are coming from. And finally, she helps you remember that the toughest ones need you the most. Each chapter has a relatable story and takeaways you can apply to your own teaching situation. The book ends with a list of key things teachers shouldn't be without, and a collection of "You Can't Make This Stuff Up" classroom stories that will remind you why you chose this profession.

Perfect to read on your own or in book studies, this isn't a research-and strategy-filled resource to tell you how to improve; it's a heartfelt look at effective ways to reach teenagers and a reminder of the huge difference you're making as a teacher!

Pamela Jean Matusz is in her 15th year as a teacher in New Jersey.

T0386607

Also Available from Routledge Eye on Education

www.routledge.com/k-12

What Great Teachers Do Differently, 3e:
Nineteen Things That Matter Most
Todd Whitaker

Thank You, Teacher: 100 Uplifting and
Affirming Letters from Your Fellow Educators
Brad Johnson and Hal Bowman

Passionate Learners: How to Engage and
Empower Your Students
Pernille Ripp

Safe, Seen, and Stretched in the Classroom:
The Remarkable Ways Teachers Shape Students' Lives
Julie Hasson

Tenaciously Teaching Teenagers

Stories and Strategies for Reaching Even the Toughest Students with Humor, Love, and Respect

Pamela Jean Matusz

Routledge
Taylor & Francis Group

NEW YORK AND LONDON

Designed cover image: © Justin Pumfrey / Getty Images

First published 2024
by Routledge
605 Third Avenue, New York, NY 10158

and by Routledge
4 Park Square, Milton Park, Abingdon, Oxon, OX14 4RN

Routledge is an imprint of the Taylor & Francis Group, an informa business

© 2024 Pamela Jean Matusz

The right of Pamela Jean Matusz to be identified as author of this work
has been asserted in accordance with sections 77 and 78 of the Copyright,
Designs and Patents Act 1988.

Library of Congress Cataloging-in-Publication Data
Names: Matusz, Pamela Jean, author.
Title: Tenaciously teaching teenagers: stories and strategies for reaching
even the toughest students with humor, love, and respect/
Pamela Jean Matusz.
Description: New York, NY: Routledge, 2023. |
Identifiers: LCCN 2022061736 | ISBN 9781032440446 (hardback) |
ISBN 9781032432557 (paperback) | ISBN 9781003370161 (ebook)
Subjects: LCSH: Teenagers–Education. | High school teachers–Humor. |
Middle school teachers–Humor. | Teenagers–Social conditions. |
Teacher-student relationships. | Classroom management.
Classification: LCC LB1607 .M36 2023 | DDC 373.11–dc23/eng/20230322
LC record available at https://lccn.loc.gov/2022061736

ISBN: 978-1-032-44044-6 (hbk)
ISBN: 978-1-032-43255-7 (pbk)
ISBN: 978-1-003-37016-1 (ebk)

DOI: 10.4324/9781003370161

Typeset in Palatino
by Deanta Global Publishing Services, Chennai, India

There are too many faces and names to dedicate this book to. Thank you to all of my students, who have taught me so much. You are all the reason why I love what I do.

I hope you all know that you have always stayed with me, even if not physically.

Thank you to Diij, a kid, a friend, and beautiful energy.

Finally, Lyle, I hope one day you will think of your mama as a woman who lives her life by the measure of how she can help others with a passion for teaching, passion for helping others, passion for learning new things, and a passion for making the world a little better for you to grow up in. I can only hope that you will find the same amount of passion and fulfillment in your chosen path.

Contents

About the Author

Pamela maintains her moxie teaching middle schoolers in New Jersey. Her enthusiasm to spend her days in precarious pandemonium further fortifies her beliefs in the teenage species. Each day she can be seen smiling as students enter her classroom and no one can predict her fierce durability. One day though, she hopes to retire from teaching so that she can enjoy her family and pursue her unending curiosity about the world around her. Nevertheless, she is already resigned to the fact that the middle school humor that she has been endowed with will not be left behind with her teaching career. Still, she is loved by her husband and her son, who will always remain her paragon of human potential.

Preface

I write this as a necessity, not as teacher of the year, or even as a great teacher at all. Teaching has become so devalued and under-appreciated. People decide to spend their lives teaching the children of strangers. This, to me, will always be mind boggling and commendable.

I see way too many bad teachers teaching and good teachers leaving. When you leave your heart in the classroom every day, it can become just too much to bear when society begins to toss false accusations your way.

I hope this book reaches those who are considering leaving the profession they once loved or those new teachers who are shiny and overly confident. Remember, only bad teachers stop learning how to be better.

In the chapters that follow, I take you inside my classroom and share stories on ways I've connected with my students, including by earning respect, by giving students a voice, and by teaching, not penalizing. At the end of each chapter, I include a practical use activity as if I were delivering this as a professional development session. If you are at a school, tell your administration this book is even better in person! To train tenacious teachers at your school contact me through my website at www.tenaciouslyteachingteenagers.com or Pamela@tenaciouslyteachingteenagers.com. In-person staff training is offered at various levels, lengths, and grades.

I

Classroom Culture

1

Do You Earn Respect?

I ask this question on the first or second day of school every year. Two reasons why I lead with this: First, it begins the dialogue of how I set expectations for behavior in my class; second, it gives my kids a voice right from the jump. They get the message that I value their opinion and want to hear what they have to say. Though this may seem like common sense, think about the first two days of your classes. Do you "stand and deliver" the entire time? Are you up at the helm preaching rules and regulations? Bringing the discussion to the kids sets the tone for the class style that they are entering. Let's face it, everyone likes to hear themselves speak, and teenagers often enjoy persuading others to agree with them. This is a multifaceted strategy (though I hate the word strategy) that will begin to set the foundation for the climate of your classroom.

Here's how this works:

Write the question on the board and tell students that they have four minutes (or any other amount of time) to think and write down their opinion. I highly recommend that you begin each class with a student-lead or student-oriented task, so this is also a great way to set the routine for the classroom structure as well. You can tell students that they will be asked to reflect on a quote or a question as a part of each class. I like to have them use a "Journal" or "Do Now" notebook or section of a binder to keep these responses organized.

DOI: 10.4324/9781003370161-2

Now, with any effective lesson, just as a courtroom lawyer will never ask a question of a witness that they don't already know the answer to, you need to know what you plan on "landing" on as the purpose of this question. The purpose of this question should be to explain that you do not need to earn the respect of others, but instead you should always lead with respect. Therefore, your classroom management is RESPECT. You give it and you expect to receive it. Now, this concept is completely baseless if you do not model it after this activity. I firmly believe that my leading with respect has been the key to my success in classroom discipline. Do not confuse respect with chaos; I respect my parents, law enforcement, college professors, etc. Therefore, I wouldn't assume that I could be rude or dismissive toward them; however, I still believe that I had the freedom and the space for my own voice to be heard in their company. Respect is the bottom line in classroom management. If a teacher does not lead with this concept, I guarantee that they will be challenged throughout the year. Students are not living in a bubble, they have every reason not to like someone who is condescending toward them, just as we would do. They may not cause trouble in your room, but a student will not engage in lessons or do work at a high level for teachers whom they don't "like." I want to clarify that this is not a popularity contest, and the adult in the room should command a level of authority. However, barking orders and demanding something that the students do not feel you give in return will be the reason why you can't understand why your class will not get "on board" throughout the year.

The Takeaway

- ◆ Treat others the way you want to be treated. Just because you are an educator by trade does not mean that your social practices go out the window. Yes, at our age we have more wisdom, and it is our job to keep order to ensure a learning environment. Yet, if I were at the store and the cashier yelled at me, "Step up to the register, you're next!" I may put my things down and leave. However, if the same scenario resulted in the cashier saying, "Excuse me, I'm open if you are ready," I will realize I wasn't paying attention and meekly approach the register.

Your ego cannot come from your profession. One day a student of yours may go on to become a Nobel Prize winner as a professor. Just because you are the teacher in the present does not mean that you are more worthy or more valuable than the humans you are teaching.

2

Making Yourself Human

We've all seen those clever coffee mugs that say something like, "Instant Human Just Add Coffee." Well, I like to think that when teaching, we become instant humans when we add humility.

This is the reason why I suggest you add some humility to your persona in the classroom:

You are in front of the classroom and the students have handed in their classwork, but it is not completed to the high standards that you have set for them. It's been a long day and you are beginning to get frustrated by what you believe is a lack of effort for their work in your class. I think if we are honest with ourselves, we've all been there as a teacher at some point. Teenagers are hard!

Now, you decide to command their attention and you go on a tangent about effort, laziness, disrespect for your lesson, etc. While you are disciplining the class, or as I call it the "come to Jesus" talk, you have the students completely silent – they were told to stop what they were doing and place all eyes on you (except for the one or two who may feel like this is the time to peacefully protest you with their eye-rolling that they seem to perfect sometime around 7th grade). Now, you are getting a little bit louder and are clearly disappointed (the best word to use). As you are pointing your finger and speaking, your classroom phone rings and as you walk over to answer it you trip over one

DOI: 10.4324/9781003370161-3

of the many obstacles in a classroom and fall – or catch yourself right before you do.

How awful. The students are going to laugh, because, let's be honest, as humans we would probably find the humor in that scenario as well. However, as a teacher you have let your ego get so big that you don't laugh with them; instead, you begin yelling at the students who did laugh and maybe even threaten them (horrible word) with a disciplinary action.

Reflecting on the situation, you were too proud to see that the situation was, indeed, a bit humorous. Unfortunately, you have built yourself up on a "I am a teacher" pedestal, and, so now, something like tripping over a book bag is a threat to your divine status!

Flip the script by adding some humility to yourself in the beginning of the year and, perhaps ideally, throughout the year as well. You'd be amazed by how much more respect you'll get from your teenagers when you allow them to peek behind the teacher "cape" and reveal your humanity.

This is what I do, and there are many ways to do this so adapt it to your personality. The point of this strategy is to relax and be an imperfect human who happens to have become a teacher; thus, it should be fun and enjoyable. I like to step off my pedestal on day one. It can easily be woven into your *Do You Earn Respect* activity. I usually say something like this:

> *I am a teacher, yes, however I am also a 36-year-old mom and woman who is still trying to figure things out. So, when I misspell things, or if I trip over my long "giraffe legs," you can correct me or giggle. I am your teacher, but as I said, I am not better than you. I am human, I was not born with a gradebook in my hand, so understand that I will respect you and that's how this classroom environment will work. It's a safe place for all of us.*

Now, imagine the same scenario. My students didn't live up to my great expectations and I am disappointed. I am having a heart-to-heart with them, and I am beginning to really lay it on thick about their need to care about school and be motivated in life when my phone rings. I walk over and trip. My students and I have a rapport that can balance both things – I can speak to them about my expectations and their mistakes or my concerns, but I can also trip and be a vulnerable human being. Now, when they laugh, I laugh. I bring it back to the initial point of my rant, but they listen because they respect me. **They want to do better because they respect me.** They don't like it when I'm disappointed in them because there is a big difference between being angry and being disappointed. By this time, they know that I care about their success, not about my class assignments. Drawing this difference will make or break your rapport. You cannot fake it, so ask yourself: Are you more concerned about the *success of your students* or about them liking or completing *your* assignments?

The Takeaway

- ◆ Dictators rule through fear. Don't be a dictator, be a teacher of the people for the people. These have made the best leaders in history.

Sometimes phrases come out of a teacher's mouth that will destroy all of their hard work building their classroom environment. These are the pitfalls to avoid:

- ◆ "It's really not that hard."
- ◆ "You don't have to be a genius."
- ◆ "This is so easy, you cannot do this simple thing."
- ◆ "Even you can figure this out."
- ◆ "Once again you …."
- ◆ "You're never going to be successful."

3

Give Them a Voice

Let your students know that their voice matters and that you are interested in them as a whole student, beyond your class. This sets the foundation for them to trust you and understand that you "care" about them. When I asked my students what makes a good teacher, the number one answer given was that a good teacher "cares about us." This concept is transformative for classroom discipline and will make your day to day more enjoyable.

No matter what your subject is, you can build this into your class routine. The one major obstacle, however, is time; I lived by timers for this purpose. A simple quick write or journal question completes the task. In addition, you can skip the "written" aspect of this and just ask students to think silently for two minutes or 60 seconds and then raise their hands to share. Making the beginning of class a short share-out or discussion can build opportunities for making connections. When a student feels like they are in a space that is safe and welcoming, they can take academic risks. Now, I like to go on tangents, so the timer is for me to make sure I facilitate the discussion in the direction or toward the purpose of the day. If you think that your subject does not lend itself to a discussion like this, then I would just have a five to ten minutes' share-out every Monday about their weekend. If, at first, they are hesitant to share, share your stories. It is OK for them to listen and not share. I promise you that one of your students secretly looks forward to your weekend story. If nothing

DOI: 10.4324/9781003370161-4

else, you have successfully made yourself a "human" and not just a teacher, and this goes a very long way for secondary students.

The Takeaways

♦ Students need routine and to feel valued. Begin each lesson with a discussion-based activity that makes personal connections to students. This creates buy-in from them because you have already shown how it connects in a meaningful way to their lives!

For example, I may not find number lines (math) or timelines (history or novels) interesting; however, if a teacher asks me to think about and share an early childhood memory that I would consider significant in my life – now I'm interested.

Then the lesson asks students to create a timeline of your life using at least five events. This sets the stage for the concept of timelines through a student-centered activity. Based on the scope of the lesson, a teacher can break this into a separate lesson on its own to introduce or conclude the concept or use it as a "starter" to begin the lesson for that day.

♦ I use my "humility" here as well and often share a funny childhood story or stories in my example timeline for the class.

4

Kids Can Hear You

I once had a colleague who was miserable. At the beginning of each day as the students were filing in and between classes all she would do is complain. She complained about her students, their work, their attitudes, their intelligence! It was draining for myself and those around her, but I'm sure it was worse for the kids. This woman wondered why her students gave her such a hard time.

Students have ears – remember that. Whether you are eating lunch in the building or in the hall on your prep, students are everywhere! They can even be there after school ends! Why in the world would you enjoy someone's company if you have heard that person bad-mouth you routinely. In fact, I think many of us would even consider confronting that colleague and asking them why they had such horrible opinions of us. If a student did that they could be expelled!

You are what you think you are. If you are miserable and hate your job and your students, tell that to a bottle of wine or a pair of running sneakers, but never broadcast that in the hallways of your school. This woman's students heard everything, and they often would pass it along to their friends if they weren't fortunate enough to hear her for themselves. Some students honestly think that some teachers "hate me." I always correct them if I hear a student say that; however, this colleague made it really difficult.

DOI: 10.4324/9781003370161-5

The Takeaways

♦ Never assume that a student is not within earshot. You'd be amazed the places students have picked things up from or just how good their hearing is. If you wouldn't want the student to know it or if you wouldn't say it in that manner to their guardians, then don't say it that way.

Be a nice human being. Even at their worst, they are someone's children and grandchildren. You are an adult, so act like it.

♦ Remember, teenagers are somewhat programmed to view their lives in an "us vs. them" scenario with all adults or authority figures. If you are thinking the student you are speaking about is not around to hear you, consider that every student will take offense to an adult criticizing a peer. Maybe the one you were speaking badly about didn't hear you, but those who do will immediately lose their respect for you. This also goes for bashing their generation as a whole.

5

Humor In Kind

It is a debatable tactic that some professionals preach to stay away from. If you do not know how you come across if you think you are being sarcastic, then do not accidentally insult your students! Having said that, if you feel in control of your humor and it is well meaning and not offensive or hurtful, I find this to be my secret weapon.

I think many of us can relate to a person who tends to be self-aware or a bit self-disparaging. To me, this is my go-to technique to assuage a defiant student. It's hard for a student to be rude or disrespectful when you beat them to it.

If I have a student who is being disruptive, I read the class to see what my best strategy is, and oftentimes teachers already know the personalities in the class. If done in front of the class, I can either build off of it at my own expense or when I address them one-on-one, I will use humor as seen in the previous scenario where I added that I was embarrassed to admit how much thought and work I put into the lesson that the student apparently thought was pointless.

Here's a quick example. If a student has their feet up on the chair in front of them and I want them to put them down, or if they're slouched over in a way that I want to correct, it often goes like this:

Me: Student A, are you comfortable?

DOI: 10.4324/9781003370161-6

Usually, students will correct themselves immediately because they understood what I was referring to. Other times they say, "Yes," and do not move. In this case I may say,
Me: Student A, are you comfortable?
Student A: Yes (no movement to correct the action).
Me: Well, that's not allowed, I'm sorry, can you please take your feet off the chair and sit up? No one is allowed to be happy or comfortable in my classroom at any time. I'm going to need you to never do that again.

This is the type of response that the students love because they think either I'm weird or I'm funny. Either way it's a win for me because the behavior is corrected in a respectful way.

Sometimes I take it even further when I have a great group.

Me: Student A, are you comfortable?
Student A: Yes (no movement to correct the action)
**Me*:* Oh, good, is there anything I can get you? A hot towel or a glass of sparkling water? Would you like a blanket?

Now, this isn't something that I would do on the first day, but my persona has shown by now and again that it is all done with respect. I smile and maybe wink or say, "come on, you're making me jealous. I want to nap too!" It's all about the delivery. I have found that with males especially, this little sprinkle of humor can go a long way in earning you some respect and avoiding defiance. Now, what do you do if the student takes you up on your offer and doesn't move?

You ask them quietly (even if you kneel down next to their desk) to *Step into Your Office* for a moment.

The Takeaways

♦ Never should the use of humor be able to be interpreted as mocking a student. I keep my humor on myself so it could never be construed that way. Also, please know which students enjoy this camaraderie and which ones are more likely to be sensitive to it. It's never at the sacrifice of a caring and safe classroom environment.

Though we feel the pressures of the standardized tests and the huge scope and sequence of our curriculums, remember that some situations just aren't that serious. At one point, this was the job that you wanted, maybe even your dream career. What happens along the way that we begin to struggle to find happiness? Every now and again, it is OK to lighten up the mood. This shows your students a "human" side as well. Embrace being weird, eccentric, or silly. It only makes it easier for you and you may even find yourself laughing throughout your day! You have to be there – why not enjoy it?

♦ Nicknames – students love them. Assuming they are not in any way derogatory, when you have a nickname for a student, it makes them feel seen. Over the years I have made a point to come up with a nickname for some students. Some are obvious; for others, I choose the students who fly under the radar because they are always on task. By giving them a fun nickname, it communicates to them that I do see them. Additionally, if a student is "not popular" in class, a cool nickname brings them into your sphere of acceptance and can really go a long way for that student.

6

Late, Missing, or Absent, Oh My!

Every district has its own policy for late work; however, they often allow the teacher to use their discretion for their own class policies.

Chasing down students who have been absent or have yet to turn in a missing assignment can be really tough and exhausting. At the elementary level, teachers are responsible for a single class of students, no more than 30 usually. As a secondary teacher we can have hundreds of students each semester. One district I taught in had a schedule of A Day and B Day. That meant that I saw each class every other day. It was great in a way because I had to plan only two lessons a week, but it was a nightmare for late work or especially absent students whom I may have had to go a week without teaching because of the schedule. If a student was absent for three days, I never saw them. If they were on a class trip or if we had an assembly, I may have seen them only one day that week.

I had six history classes – three 80-minute classes per day, alternating days. Each class averaged about 30 students, which meant I had about 175 students. That is 175 essays, 175 HW assignments, and every assignment left me with 175 submissions. My motto was always this: They (the students) had only five teachers that semester, I had 175 of them. If they were absent, it was on them to make sure they caught up on what they missed.

DOI: 10.4324/9781003370161-7

I wasn't chasing down students when I could barely remember their names, never mind the days they were out!

This is my system, and it has been pretty successful. Every teacher has their own preferences and routines, but if this is a yearly struggle for your class, then try this on for size.

First, on the first day of school or on the first day of a new marking period or semester (which is an awesome time to fix strategies that weren't working … just say you've been waiting until the second half of the year to prepare them for the next grade, etc.), I tell my students that they must manage their absent work. I have a hanging folder in my room with several slots – at least seven is best. Five of these slots have a folder with a day of the week written on the tab, Monday to Friday. When the student returns from being out, they go to the folder and find the days of the week when they were out and look in the folder to grab the materials that were handed out. If we took notes, there will be a copy of those notes. If we took a test, there will be a list of names that need to see me to make arrangements for the test makeup.

   Step 1: Make it the job of someone else – delegation of duty as
      I like to think of it.

Even in high school, there is a student who wants to be needed, helpful, organized, or even wants to be a teacher. This is your best friend. In the beginning of the year ask someone to be your TA, or teaching assistant. Their job is the following:

- ◆ Each class write a list of absent students.
- ◆ Take an extra copy of any assignments passed out during class.
- ◆ If taking notes, turn their notes in to be copied at the end of class.
- ◆ Place collected papers in the "What Did I Miss?" folder.
- ◆ Place the list of absent students on my desk.
- ◆ They are also the "go-to" for any questions about what we did that day.

This job places the responsibility for all missing or absent work squarely on the shoulders of the student. It teaches them independence and ownership of their decisions. If a student is absent or missed a class for any reason, they are aware that they are to come to me for questions only if they were not answered by the "What Did I Miss" folder or the class TA.

The next step is also critical:

Step 2: Makeup Work Bin

I have "mom-brain" and had it way before I became a mother. I make it very clear to my students that if they ever hand me late or missing work, I will lose it. In fact, I believe I tell them that they might as well light a fire and use it to roast marshmallows. I cannot keep track of who hands me what, especially with secondary students who love to make every assignment a beach mystery novel by not putting their name on ANYTHING.

So, I own my weakness, and I created a late/missing work bin. No matter if it was missing from being absent, late because they decided not to do it when I assigned it, or a baby pterodactyl took it, it goes in the bin. It can be two days late or 25 days late. It all goes in the same darn bin. Now, my only responsibility is to check the bin at the end of each day and enter the grades into the corresponding place in my gradebook, with or without a "late" date of submission. I always include the due date of the assignments in the assignment description, so by entering the date submitted, both the student and the guardian can see how long it took to turn in.

Now, you may be wondering, but what is the point deduction for late work or the days given for late work? I have changed this protocol based on the district. However, this is what I have learned about secondary students – either they care or they don't. The ones who will take advantage of the policy will turn in their work within a week or two. The ones who do not care about their missing work will never turn it in. Therefore, I can tell students that I have the most generous late-work policy and will accept all late work for half credit (50/100) until the end of the semester. First, this seems really awesome, but, in actuality, I am giving students a 50% whether it is three days late or 60 days late. Unless they were absent, of course, for which they usually have as many days as they were out to complete the work they missed.

On the surface, this policy seems extremely gracious, and it is. Instead of a zero, they get 50 points. Yet, it is a very strict, no-nonsense message that late work will never be beneficial. A 50/100 is much better than a zero (50 times better of course); however, depending on the weight of the classwork category, this can really affect a final grade. When a parent reaches out with concerns over a student's grade, it really helps to explain that "I accept all late assignments as long as they are handed in before the end of the marking period, most teachers only give students a few days." This sounds extremely reasonable and often assuages their anger. Imagine being able to tell a parent that their student handed in an assignment two MONTHS late and you still gave them half credit? That is a power move for you, and parents are usually appreciative.

How does this policy change by district? If you teach in a district that has only two marking periods or semesters, you can do the math and calculate the mid-semester or mid-marking period date and apply the same policy. However, accepting work up to five months late as opposed to two and a half months can really be a paperwork nightmare and cause major complacency among the students. If this is the case in your district, I'd encourage you to use the mid-semester/marking period technique. I taught in a district for years that had four marking periods and this policy worked like a gem. Honestly, very few students took advantage of it, which was sad, but it made them accountable for their poor decisions when addressing any concerns about their grades. As I said, I have at least 125 of them, sometimes more, so it was their responsibility to take the initiative to find, complete, and turn in work that was missed.

Remember, if you choose to use this, reward that TA for taking on a major responsibility to make your life easier.

The Takeaways

♦ If you use this that means you need to always make sure you have extra copies in case they are needed for the folder. Also, if it is an electronic assignment, it should auto grade for a zero or missing until they complete it. Adjust the grade as needed. Also, for assessments, I do not take the 50% penalty.

♦ If you use this policy, make it known! Parents and guardians have a difficult time criticizing such a generous policy. It makes the students' lack of effort the focal point, though, sadly, they often do not take advantage of it.

7

Safe from Reading

I was normally a great reader, in fact, I loved reading to the class. I have always volunteered for something ever since I can remember. I think at first it was the rush of learning to read and loving the process. Maybe in a way, I loved the sound of my voice filling the room. I was never one to shy away from speaking in front of others.

This day was the same as always. Honors English freshman year, we were reading the *Odyssey*, a very out-of-date epic that Homer has haunted us for thousands of years after his time. I was reading a part, I forget which one, but I think maybe the anticipation of knowing when I was going to read became overwhelming. This anticipation anxiety kicked in and all of a sudden I was standing up at my desk, book in hand, gasping for breath through what seemed like an invisible, but quite rigid, straw.

I know my peers could hear the octaves of my voice rising as my breathing shallowed … more … and more … until I felt like I was going to pass out. I was horrified. This never happened to me before. I redeemed myself and my reputation by immediately volunteering to read another part again. I was too young to realize what I was doing, but I was "getting right back on the horse," so that my momentary fear didn't become a phobia.

Very rarely did I experience this type of anxiety when speaking or reading again. However, that memory is from 1999, and clearly it had an impact.

DOI: 10.4324/9781003370161-8

Due to my own experience, I never "cold call" on a student to read in my class. First, this may cause a lot of unnecessary distress for students who are not great readers or for students who like to read but are shy. In your mind, you have to imagine the cost over the benefit.

1. Good reader/ shy and hates reading in front of peers.
2. Bad reader/ doesn't want to be exposed by reading out loud.
3. Bad reader/ likes to read out loud and peers snicker or laugh at their mistakes making them very self-conscious.
4. Good reader/ loves to read out loud.

If these are the scenarios that are possible for reading in class, then you can rest assured that the great readers who enjoy reading to the class *will be the ones volunteering without any risk*. Therefore, there is no need to call on the students with their hands down. If they wanted to read or felt confident enough, they would have their hands raised to volunteer. What possible benefit could outweigh the risk of a panic attack? If you want to assess their reading skills, do it privately in small groups of similar skills sets, or one on one. Whole class exposure will not even provide an accurate assessment if the student is already nervous.

For this reason, I will never, ever, call on a student who has not volunteered to read or assign parts to random students. There was a popular technique called "round robin" when I was in school. Each student would get a paragraph to read and the process would roll along in the order of our seats. When the person in front of me stopped, my turn was next, and then the student behind me, and so on. This is the same thing as calling on someone who has not raised their hand to read. First off, most students count ahead to figure out which paragraph they will be reading. Then, more often than not, this student practices reading their "assigned" paragraph. Now, you have not only a nervous student, but also one who is not even listening to the text being read. This defeats the entire purpose of reading as a class.

I think this concept may be hard for ELA teachers to grasp because they may very well love to read and have never been the student who was terrified to read. Another unwanted effect of the "round robin" or cold call reading is the amount of students who will use the hall pass to avoid their turn. Weak or shy readers will often try to leave the room for any reason for fear of reading in front of their peers. Now, you have students who are not even present for the lesson because of their fear of reading.

The Takeaway

♦ The strategies that force students who have not volunteered to read will ultimately defeat the purpose of its function and possibly even deter students from enjoying your class. Is the purpose of an educator to make sure every student enjoys your class? No. But should an educator knowingly make a student feel uncomfortable in their class? No. Rethink the old practices. Intentionally make each student in your class feel safe – even if that means safe from reading out loud.

8

Writing Utensil Cat'astrophe

Let's face it, teenagers could care less about writing utensils. As a teacher, this can add up to a mountain of unnecessary annoyance and spending of our own money if we choose to supply them with pencils.

I accidentally came across two great things: cat pens and a manual pocket-sized pencil sharpener.

First, do yourself a favor and order a box of golf pencils. This is a pretty common teacher hack. They are small and not very fun to write with. Any time a student does not have a pen or pencil, give them a golf pencil – eventually they'll ask their peers instead of you.

One year my electric pencil sharpener bit the dust. Students kept walking up to it in class and then asking me if I had another sharpener. I, of course, decided to be witty about it. I took a hand-held manual pencil sharpener and put it on the ledge of the whiteboard. Above it I drew an arrow and wrote, "High-tech pencil sharpener." Why was this effective? It was great because it not only made the kids laugh, but it was also QUIET! Now, if a student had to sharpen their pencil in the middle of a lesson it was not a disruption to me. After this year, I would continue to use this trick and just told the students that my mechanical pencil sharpener broke. Students didn't want to do the work of sharpening their pencil in front of the class unless it was really necessary, and if they did make a show of it, I'd stop talking and

DOI: 10.4324/9781003370161-9

just look at them. The class would follow until they realized and that usually stopped any unnecessary performances.

Standing on line at the local dollar store trying to manage my six-year-old son, I spotted hideous pens and immediately thought, "I need those in my classroom." The pens had little plush cat heads on the top. I bought ten and decided that this would end the struggle with kids not having their writing utensils. I put six of them up on the whiteboard with a magnetic clip and above them I wrote, "Writing Utensil Cat'astrophe." Students who had nothing to write with were allowed to take a cat, of course they were given names, and they had to return them at the end of class. I could easily see if one was missing when they were up on the board, and, also, it was just fun to ask students if they were trying to steal my cat, Waffles.

As usual, I thought no teenager would want to be caught dead using these pens, but they became extremely sought after. I had to replace them frequently. Nothing against the dollar store, but the pens ran out of ink quickly, and, when they did, I'd replace them after letting the student know that they killed my cat. It was an easy joke and a manageable way to keep track of the pens I loaned out. This scenario gave many opportunities for light-hearted jokes, and coming up with names for the cats was my favorite part. Eventually, the students were fully invested in the joke and would randomly tell me that my cat was "dying" while taking notes or that they thought they may have "killed" my cat. Of course, we had to draw a tombstone above that cat and have a moment of silence. These are the little things that students will appreciate and remember for years after they had you as a teacher.

The Takeaway

♦ Some teachers take points off for not having a pen or a pencil, to me this is just a condescending action. How many times have we misplaced a pen or pencil? It's part of the human experience, and, at the end of the day, not only do I not have time to track deducted points for a pen, but

I also trust that my students appreciate that I choose my battles. If you have no writing utensil and you are chewing gum, then I'll give you a pen, but spit out your gum. If you have your feet up on the desk and are chewing gum, then spit out your gum and sit correctly. If you are chewing gum and you are also on task, then chew away – quietly. I never spell this out for them explicitly; however, they begin to notice the trend. Respect is what I am looking for. If you are going to ask for a favor, then you had better make sure you are doing all the things that you are expected to do. On the other hand, if you are a rock star in my class, then I do not see the bright green gum you've been chewing quietly. An early lesson on how the real world works.

9

Accent'uate Your Lessons

Okay, I may lose even the most adventurous teachers in this chapter, but it is worth it. One day when I was a substitute, way before I got a tenured position, I was leading a class in reading a play. I had students volunteer for the parts, and we needed one more part to be filled. Finally, after an agonizing pause, a student raised his hand. I was about to write his name next to the last character when he asked, "Can I read in an accent?" At first, I thought he was a clown and wanted to get some laughs. But he was not smiling. I asked him, "Would you prefer to read in an accent?" He nodded, "If I can read in an accent, I'll do it."

I forget what accent the student used, British or Australian, but he did it well – not the accent, the part. I was perplexed as to why offer an accent if not for humor? He read his part with the right amount of seriousness, and, after the first few lines, the class moved beyond the strange accent, and he completed the task. Since I was a substitute, I was unable to track him down later on to ask him about his idea. Many days later, it hit me. He was nervous. The student was nervous to read in front of the class, but if he did it with an accent, it gave him a sort of alias. If he stumbled over his lines, *it wasn't him*, it was the Aussie. What a beautifully genius move!

As a substitute, you get to work in the "lab" of education. I honestly attribute my years of subbing to my eclectic style of teaching. First, it made me refine my class management to a

DOI: 10.4324/9781003370161-10

fine-tipped weapon if necessary. Second, I got to observe different class rules, climates, and styles of teaching. I was able also to try out new ideas, it wasn't my class after all, if it failed terribly. I didn't have a permanent consequence. I would learn and begin to build an arsenal of beauty – beautiful tips, tricks, and styles that were the best of all my experiential teaching and observations around the school. Very rarely can a person who wants to be a teacher get an opportunity to see examples of so many teaching styles. I could be the music teacher one day, a physical education teacher the next, and end with being the math teacher for the week! Each set of subplans left were like little roadmaps to the classroom culture. Some rooms ran like a well-oiled machine, and all I had to do was supervise. Others behaved like mom and dad had left for the weekend and the babysitter had no directions.

Each day was a learning opportunity, and I really am not sure if I'd do what I do without the experience. At the time, I was bummed about not being able to find a permanent position. Yet, looking back, I realize I took advantage of the best teaching program one could get. College was great, but nothing prepares a teacher like having to be quick on your feet and survive middle school kids who celebrate when they see a substitute in the room (and not because they liked me).

With this unique opportunity, I tried out the accent theory I had. This time, when asking for volunteers to read, I would offer it as an option straight away. This did not seem to work very well. I tried asking a student to use an accent while they were reading. This also was not successful. Finally, I found my approach. I would begin reading in an accent. Students were, of course, alarmed and amused, but this seemed to break the ice and soon students would follow suit. With that came more volunteers.

The Takeaways

♦ To this day I will use this in my class. Sometimes just to shake it up so my poor students don't have to hear the same voice all class. Other times, just to get those slouching heads up and looking around in confusion. Either way, it's worth a try "mate."

♦ Maybe this isn't something you do during the first week of school or maybe that is the ideal time to rope in the kids. Either way, all teachers should have a funny voice or an accent in their drawer of tricks. Teaching is often compared to acting or performing, and we have to admit that, to some extent, we need to embrace and empower that aspect of the profession.

II

Movement in the Classroom and into the Community

10

Learning in Motion

One of the best compliments that I received during an observation from my administrator was when I stopped mid-lesson and told my students to stand up.

I forget what exactly I was teaching, but it was the class directly after lunch and the kids were zoned out. I was not happy with their lack of participation while being observed. Instead of calling them out on having no energy (a not so great tactic for teenagers), I stopped teaching and told them to all stand up and push in their chairs. "Stand behind your chairs. Do what I say and not what I do." I then played a version of Simon Says, but I would eventually do something opposite of what I said and inevitably students would mimic my moves and not listen to what I said. I do this a lot to get them up and awake. After about three two-minute rounds of this game, I had them sit down and I continued the lesson.

After class my supervisor came over to me, "That brain break was really good. I could tell that the kids were not really in the lesson. It just goes to show that you had your finger on the pulse of the room. It was really impressive." Now, I think all teachers do something similar, but it made me a feel a certain way that my administrator didn't see it as a weakness, but a strength. After that day I realized that using the tricks I had tucked up my sleeve was always a good idea – even during an observation. I was afraid that I would be criticized for using instructional time

DOI: 10.4324/9781003370161-12

to play a game, but, instead, I was praised for realizing my class needed to wake up.

Brain breaks are a necessity. If you have had the privilege of sitting through a professional development session, or staff meeting, you are aware of how we can all become restless after only a few minutes of sitting. Some get lethargic, some are antsy. Either way, no one is very comfortable and often we are all zoning out or doing something else. Imagine if you couldn't have your cell phone, laptop, or talk to a colleague next to you during one of these scenarios. I know I would struggle not using the time to multitask schoolwork and listening.

Our students would be disciplined by their teacher for doing any of those three things during whole-class instruction. Not only is that a big ask for adults, but also imagine a teenager who is accustomed to being entertained constantly via their devices! The attention span is not conducive to lectures these days.

I once read a study that suggested that physical activity was the best way to wake yourself up, more effective than a cold shower and coffee. So when I see my kids begin to zone out, I make them move! Just like my musical notes, any movement is much appreciated by the kiddos, and it is not a very tough thing to incorporate. In fact, it could cost a simple five dollars.

I went to the store, Five Below, and purchased a rubber hexagonal ball. I labeled on each side a quick exercise: jumping squats, wall-sits, push-ups, etc. I decided this would be an easy way to incorporate a brain break in my class. So I keep it within reach and when I see the kids' eyes starting to glaze over, I take it out. "Everyone stand up behind your chair." I tell them that they do not have to do the activity that is rolled; however, they must stand up until the time is up. I offer the alternative of jumping jacks or stretching as well. I find that most kids actually like the physical challenge. I always do it with them, but it is not necessary for this to be useful. Twenty-five jumping lunges, 60 second wall-sits, 25 triceps dips on the edge of their chairs, 60 seconds of push-ups. I put tape over the "water break" and "sit-ups" option so that we are not on the floor or leaving the room. When I roll those, I allow a student to choose any activity. There has been more than one instance where the one-minute wall sit became a competition for a Jolly Rancher. I make sure I correct their posture and check their form so that it is a real challenge. In my experience, only a handful of students choose to do an alternative activity. But just standing gets their blood flowing and it is better than sitting for that minute. I've had students request these challenges, and I tell them that if we get through the lesson to a certain point, then I will let them roll it. It is a good motivational tool and a great way to wake up the kiddos too.

Not all activities have to be so short. I read yet another study that suggested physical movement actually helps keep information in our short-term memory for a tad bit longer. So what did I do? I created review relays! These are exactly what they sound like – a relay race to review for a test.

I like skills that do not require much athleticism but a lot of movement. I have one person on each team who does the "thinking" and not the moving. I randomly number off teams and take the class outside. Depending on the class, and I think we teachers all have a pretty good idea of who our students are, I design the course. Maybe it's about 20-foot intervals. If they are much more enthusiastic, I switch up the relay movement. However, it is usually the same thing. I ask a question and the "knowledge-keeper" tells their first teammate the answer, that teammate runs, karaoke, crab-crawls, etc. to the next teammate and relays the answer. The last teammate has to run the full length of the race back to me and give me the correct answer.

This works well because my high-energy kids can get all of their energy out, and everyone has a part. One year I took my class out to the soccer field behind my school and set them up for a relay. Every line on the field a student stood ready to receive and relay the answer. This class was particularly into the relay challenge and so we had a lot of fun. Each student chose which leg of the relay they wanted to do for their team. One round we had a bear-crawl, a crab-crawl, a backwards trot and a full-out sprint toward me to give the answer. There were plenty of times when a student was faster, but had the wrong answer. In fact, I've had two or three students cross the line with a wrong answer and the fourth place team take the win because it centers around the answer, not the speed. It requires teamwork, each student must remember and clearly repeat the answer they were given. Only the "knowledge-keeper" hears the question from me in a huddle, then they run a very short distance (ten feet) and give the answer to the first leg. Therefore, if they do not work together, speed, athleticism, and knowledge will all break down if they do not communicate well.

If I have extra students who want only to answer a question, then they can take turns for their team, or I have "line-watchers" who make sure that the next leg of the relay stays on their line until they get the answer. They also help me watch the finish line and decide who was first. With this format, all students can be involved no matter their personality. It is always a nice change from the typical review session in a classroom. I cannot tell you how many times a student would come back to school the next day and tell me how they explained our review to their family that night. They explain what happened in class with such excitement because it is usually something they have never done before. This is often when I get those emails from parents who explain to me that their son always hated ELA or history class, but now how he talks about it so enthusiastically.

The Takeaways

- ◆ Not everyone is into reading, poetry, essays, or ancient societies. I find that my male students especially do not enjoy writing. Put them on a field and tell them to run their fastest or have them do triceps dips in class – it's amazing how movement can make or break a student's tolerance for a class. It's free, and it's not hard to do.
- ◆ Search "Wheel of Names" on the Internet or something similar. There are many free apps that enable you to create a wheel to spin, and maybe that is the movement for the day or the bonus if students finish their work with time left in class. I have made up review games that consisted of three wheels, and one was just a funny grumpy cat with hilarious music. We were all cracking up laughing each time a student landed on it.

11

Musical Notes and Softly Hitting School Property

Despite the attempts of even the most entertaining educator, there will be lessons that require the student to complete an assignment that may cause their eyes to roll to the back of their heads. As a history teacher, I had many classes that required students to take notes. I loved peppering in information about the topic as they copied names, wars, or cultures on their papers. However, believe it or not, my students did not always think these lessons were all that fun.

I decided to shake it up. My district used a note-taking paper format that required students to interact with their notes. On the left side of the paper there was a column for students to pull out questions from their notes (questions that are answered in the notes) and to also write a summary of their notes (answer those questions in a statement). I saw this as an opportunity to move and shake the note-taking around – literally.

I'd have students take out their note paper, and, since it was a district format, they already knew how to interact with their notes. So I would have students copy my notes or my PPT onto their note paper. I always told them that their notes could look however they wanted them to look. Most learners, especially those visual learners, know what works for them. I am not grading them on the exactness of their notes or the format. I am

DOI: 10.4324/9781003370161-13

walking around and monitoring that they are copying the content, but maybe don't need to bullet information, or underline certain words. We all organize the schemas in our mind's eye a certain way. If my format of bullets and arrows or colors does not help but possibly even confuses or overwhelms my students, then I certainly do not want them to copy mine exactly. As long as they had the information that they needed, and could understand it well enough to do well on an open-notes test, then we were rolling in the right direction!

I began teaching with an interactive SMART board around the year 2011. This was a welcome evolution to the overhead and transparency paper I had been using prior. If you happen to have no idea what I am referring to, then you certainly must be a new and energetic teacher! One of my favorite features of this interactive board was that it was touch sensitive (though we had to recalibrate it often). This was splendid for my less than exciting note-taking sessions.

I walked around the room with one of my plushy animals (my class friends that I've mentioned), and this one was a Yankees baseball bear. As students took their notes and I walked the room, I would quietly put the bear on the desk of a student who was doing well. They were focused, notes were well written, and they weren't talking. The student already knew what this meant because I had explained it to them. The student with the bear would get to throw it at the board when everyone was done. *I knew that everyone was done when their pencils or pens were down.* I warned my doodlers that I would think they were still writing, and this would often lead to a long awkward stare until they caught on.

So now my student with the bear would get my signal and they would either stand at their desk (depending on the distance) or just throw the bear from their chair at the board. Why? Because it changed to the next slide in the PPT! Remember, it was touch sensitive! This tiny little insertion of "reckless" fun made my boring lessons fun. I also found that this would motivate a lot of my male students, who seemed to be less enthusiastic than their highlighting-color-coordinating-with-a-key-on-top-of-their-notes female peers. It encouraged engagement, and it is amazing what the permission to throw a stuffed animal at school property will do for participation. One warning – if you do try this, take the eyes and nose off. The enthusiasm shown by your student-athletes can do some damage.

Another trick I made up was called "musical notes." Just as it sounds, students moved around the room and stopped when the music stopped. They would then sit down at the desk near them (not their own) and interact with those students' notes.

Now, this will really ruffle the feathers of your note-taking perfectionists. You know the ones I am talking about, the ones with the white-out sitting on their desk next to the stack of colored pens or highlighters. However, sometimes in life we have to stop trying to be perfect. This was the time for my students.

The Takeaways

♦ Depending on my class and the length of the notes I would decide at different points when to play musical notes. Usually, it was when all the notes were copied for the lesson. Remember, our district had a format that required students to "pull out" or write questions down in the left margin based on the content of the notes. So I'd play music and my students would walk around with a writing utensil until the music stopped. Sometimes I would have them walk backwards, or sideways, or like an Egyptian (ancient – The Bangles). When the music stopped, they sat down at the nearest desk, and I would tell them how many questions they had to pull from the notes. In total, most notes could offer about four to six questions per side of paper. Sometimes I'd have them do all four if time was running short. Other times we would play this game to write all four questions with four differ-ent peers. It helped to stop students from just writing the same question anywhere they sat (because they would be working with a different part of the notes).

Let's not forget the summary! Then, I would do the same with the summary portion of the notes. Often I would have students return to their seats and write the summary answering the questions that were written down. We can say it was collaboration, building off of the ideas of other classmates to complete the notes. This format of note-taking actually called for the summary to be done as a "do now" or "starter" the following day. This way the students have to return to the notes and review them. I also would have them complete it as a "do now" the next day, if possible. This also works great because students think differently, and so maybe there are questions written for them to answer that they didn't think about.

◆ If musical notes are not for you, but you'd like to make changes to how students take notes in your class, try jigsaw notes. Put a different section of the notes on group tables and have the students write them on big chart paper. Then have the students hang them up in order on the walls. Either during the same lesson or the next day, the whole class can copy the notes as they move around the room. Or you can move the notes onto regular notebook paper and have each group present them to the class.

12

Put Them in the Lesson

The title of this chapter may be misleading. I am not suggesting that you cleverly add student names to worksheets, though I do love doing that if I am using worksheets in class. The kids get a real kick out of it.

As a teacher of ancient history for many years, I definitely heard students sigh when I told them what we were going to learn about. I know it is hard to believe, but these 14-year-olds didn't get enthused over the first villages or domestication of animals. So I had to make these things relatable. Many adults cannot relate to the Stone or Copper Ages, so I understood their detachment from the material. Until, that is, when I realized that I needed to *put them in the lesson*.

I had taught seventh grade ELA for three years when I got an interview for an opening in the same school for eighth grade history. I enjoyed ELA, but, at heart, I have always been a teacher of history. In my ELA class it was easy to get my students to relate to our class novels. Characters, suspense, point of view, setting, the conflict – all of the elements were read-made tools. However, ancient Pangea and Neanderthals were not so relatable. I sat at my desk that first week in my new content area racking my brain for ways to make the content interesting to a teenager who is not naturally into history. Everyone loved to learn about the ancient society of Egypt, but early man and the Stone Age were not so exciting, and it took up at least two months' worth of my

DOI: 10.4324/9781003370161-14

curriculum. I always thought outside of the box when teaching. Even in ELA I loved using music for things such as tone, mood, or poetry. I used charades for help students improve their writing. "*Show* the reader how the character feels, don't *tell* them," I'd say as I gave volunteers a card with an emotion written on it for them to portray.

It was not a huge leap for me, then, to imagine my students getting involved in the lessons. I figured the best way to teach them was to make them do it themselves. The Neanderthal unit provided me with the opportunity to teach them the importance of verbal and written communication. I would break the students into groups. Each group had one volunteer to "act." The rules were very clear, the "Neanderthal" could not spell letters in the air or mouth words or letters. They were not allowed to write anything. Letters and words simply did not exist. I then would call the group's "Neanderthal" into the hall (my office), and each one was given a uniquely challenging task to communicate to their group. I answered any questions they might have and told them the rules. At the end of each task, I incorporated something like the YMCA dance to signal to me that they had completed the task. Then the group would sit down. The first group to finish won.

So, what happened? Well, as you might imagine the "Neanderthals" went into the lesson very confidently until they realized the breakdown of communication. Some groups didn't even guess the first task. So, as designed, all of a sudden, I had eighth graders gesticulating and grunting. They all morphed into "cavemen" during the daunting task. It was quite wonderful to watch a room full of 14-year-olds becoming the exact thing that they were trying to understand in our history books. I gave them such obscure tasks, and I was always impressed by what they were able to communicate.

- ◆ Sharpen a yellow-colored pencil
- ◆ Use it to draw a squirrel
- ◆ Organize an attack on a make-believe elephant by digging a ditch and covering it with sticks (they had to correctly

communicate the strategy to their group and carry out the make-believe action)
♦ Do the YMCA

Once I saw the YMCA I knew it was time to head over to the group and ask them what the messages were. It is like a game of charades, but instead of having a handful of categories, these are very random tasks. As some students excelled, others worked tirelessly and became very discouraged. I directed them not to stop trying, no matter how far they got. I set a timer, about 15 minutes, but if a group finished, I would tell them to sit quietly after I validated their messages. This worked well because students were able to observe their peers, and observing their peers struggling to communicate was a big value for the lesson's purpose. They could see one another begin to grunt and bang things. It turned an era over hundreds of thousands of years ago that was impossible to relate to into our modern classroom.

Continuing on in the same vein, still in Prehistoric Period history, I took my kids "hunting." You see, I would split my class into "bands" of hunters. In fact, I often would let them choose their own hunting band; this made them super excited. I aimed for about six groups of five to six. Next, I had the students randomly select cards, which I preassigned "situations" to before class.

So, for example, students who pulled a Jack were assigned a different scenario from the Queen, etc. Of course, I made sure I evenly divided the cards for the experience I wanted them to have. What is a "situation" or scenario? Well, once I had them in their groups of choice, and all the cards were passed out (I made sure each group got a fresh set of cards), I then explained what we were doing.

We are going hunting today, like a band of Neanderthals. Your group is your band, just like we have been learning about. Now, I have hidden about 150 marbles outside before class. Clear marbles. There are three large marbles, the rest are standard size. These marbles are hidden all over the area outside our classroom window. When we get outside, I will show you the exact boundaries. Marbles can be found "in" a tree, "on" the ground, "in" the grass, "on" the walkway.

No marble is completely covered up; they are not meant to be extremely hard to find. This is not so much a task to *find* the marbles as it is to *get* the marbles. Each marble is worth one pound of meat, the large ones are worth five pounds. Each member of your group needs seven pounds of meat to survive the next week. Once we get back inside, you will count up your pounds and delegate the "meat" to members of your band. You may have to decide who starves if you come up short for each person. That means each group needs about 40 marbles for all of you to live. There are only 150 marbles and there are six groups of you. That means there will certainly be "deaths from starvation" in at least two groups.

Rules:

1. You may steal marbles from other bands, but you can only attack the marbles, not the individual (I then read them the riot act about appropriate conduct).
2. You may use a shirt or pockets to carry marbles collected.
3. You may find/keep as many marbles as you can, there is no limit per person.

Now: Scenarios or "Situations"

> **Ace Card**: You are free to hunt without any issues as soon as I say so.
>
> **Jack Card**: You broke your weapon in the last hunt, and so you will need to build a tower of Jenga blocks before you can begin hunting. I will supervise this.
>
> **Queen Card**: You were injured, and so you may begin hunting as soon as I say so, but you have a handicap. You must rubber band together your three fingers: middle, ring, and pinky, on both hands and keep them this way throughout the hunt. You must use your hands and nothing else to collect marbles. (Of course, I do it for them so that they do not band them too tight or too loose).

King Card: You are also injured; however, yours is a bit different. You must ONLY use two plastic spoons to pick up marbles.

Joker Card: You can only point to marbles; you CANNOT pick them up. However, you may carry them.

This is where the rules that allow them to "steal" food from peers comes into action. Students can bump a peer's spoon or try to get the marble the "Joker" points out to their band members. This will require you to really watch what is happening around you, but it is worth the experience for the kiddos.

Once you complete the hunt, the students will have to calculate the "pounds of meat" they were able to "hunt." This part of the lesson is always a bit eye-opening to me. Almost without fail, if they are short, the amount they need for the entire band, they will always vote to "starve" the member who did the least work. I have never seen a band vote a member out when necessary for any other reason. Even friends will turn on each other! It says a lot about human nature, and I wonder if it wasn't the same during the actual time in history. If a member is wounded or cannot contribute, it seems that they would likely be the first one left behind.

To bring the activity to a completion, I have students fill out a reflection the next day. Then we discuss their thoughts about the lesson, the difficulties, the decisions that they made about not having enough food, and why they made them. Finally, we discussed any strategies that they had developed to keep an edge over other bands. I draw them back to the non-verbal lesson and ask if hunting would have been easier if they had the ability to communicate. Most times they have a great attitude and really learn the lesson I was aiming to teach.

Another lesson that I used to put my kids into the content was when we were learning about the samurai culture. This one particular year I was able to get further than normal in the textbook, and so I was trying new ways to get them interested in the material. Believe it or not, not all students found samurai culture to be very interesting. Maybe their attention spans have shortened so much that the art of war is no longer of interest.

So one day I made a decision on my feet, as I often did, and took my class outside. I asked them to tell me the formalities that the samurai followed on the battlefield. Afterward, I had them line up numbering them by twos. The ones were on one side of the field, facing the twos on the opposite end. They faced each other and, on my signal, each student stepped forward and yelled out their qualifications and major accomplishments as a warrior. They were shy at first, but, as always, there was a student with true bravado who made it seem "cool." Next, on my signal they ran toward each other. They had to find a classmate who was about an even match to their height and weight, then play Rock-Paper-Scissors (RPS) best out of three. The losers sat down and then the winners continued the "battle." Eventually, there was an epic end battle of RPS that had both sides cheering on a favorite of their choice. It was always exciting, and it never required any skill or materials for the students.

Another lesson that the kids really liked was the "story" elements project. Instead of writing an entire story, students worked in groups to complete a packet brainstorming the story they would write. Plot chart, character sketches, tone, mood, theme, etc. were all explained. The only thing they did not do was actually write the story. Instead, they had a choice board and had to choose any two options to demonstrate their story.

One option was a movie trailer on iMovie or another phone app. Another option was to be interviewed "in character" or bring in a meal from the story. I gave students the option of writing a score for a scene, and my very talented student played the violin and added electronic beats in an impressive presentation. Others chose to make a 3-D model of their setting. Each choice had a written element that required them to explain the details of their choice and how it fit on the plot chart.

It was a lot of fun watching those movie trailers in class. One year I taught on a farm at a charter school and my truck was parked on the grass outside the building. Students asked if they could use my truck in the trailer. With much trust, I allowed them to get in it and pretend to be driving it, and one student managed to lodge their body so far under the front tire that I actually thought he was run over. Of course, I had the keys in my hand and was ten feet away supervising, but they were able to do amazing things with their editing tools. I was super proud of their finished product.

In a similar lesson, I was teaching *A Midsummer Night's Dream* and the eighth graders were not all that into the text. I tried to place the emphasis on the love triangle and the drama between the young adults. When I explained it this way, they did get into the plot and seemed to understand it better – or at least *want* to understand it.

Once again, I tried to bring the story into modern times in a relatable way. The class had to choose partners, two to four people, and place the four main characters involved in the love triangle into a modern setting. The names had to stay and so did the plot. It was thrilling to see Demetrius and Lysander fight over Hermia in a mock episode of *Dr. Phil*. Meanwhile, Dr. Phil had a lot to say to Helena about her sense of worth. "Is it true that you asked Demetrius to treat you like a spaniel?" The audience gasped! Most groups did a fabulous job reimagining the classic play as a modern-day *Mean Girls* or a typical high school hallway scene. Soon, Shakespeare and all of his old language was fascinating. They relished the opportunity to use Old English as modern high school students in "high school musical" reenactments.

In my freedom to pick reading materials for an eighth grade class I taught, I supplemented *All Quiet on the Western Front* with, and excerpts from, Tim O'Brien's *The Things They Carried*. At one point in the novel *All Quiet on the Western Front*, the narrator describes a merciless drill that required the men to dive under bunks over and over again. After reading this chapter, I had my students try the drill using the classroom tables. They were eager to move around, and they were able to reflect on their experience and make inferences about the experiences of the characters. Similarly, when teaching *The Things They Carried*, I had students add the pounds of all of the equipment that the average soldier was described to have had carried. We agreed it was between 50 and 60 pounds. I found a backpack, and a very awesome colleague loaned me his personal weights (don't ask me why they were in the classroom) and I had the students walk about 50 yards with the pack on.

In each of these scenarios, students could opt out and it was never a mandatory activity, though I found that only a very few chose that option. It always seemed to me that the kids loved trying new things and they enjoyed doing something so "out of the box" for classwork.

Walking with a backpack of weights for 50 yards may seem like a "waste of time" to some teachers. I would suggest that my students were much more invested in the novels because of the way they interacted with them. However, more importantly, their personal connection made their essays so much more powerful. After reading *The Things They Carried*, I gave my students a prompt to respond to:

> *As we have read in* The Things They Carried, *Vietnam soldiers carried both physical and metaphorical weight.*
> *Which of the two do you believe was more of a struggle for them; the backpacks or the mental trauma?*
> *Cite evidence from the text to support your choice.*

Most of these responses were very thought-provoking, and each choice was well defended with textual evidence. I allowed them to use a personal experience in addition to textual evidence to support their choice and these were very sobering. The teen years are often written off as the worst by adults, but I have plenty of textual evidence that would suggest otherwise.

The Takeaway

♦ I remember back in college, when I was first learning how to write lesson plans, we used the Madeline Hunter format. This format was very daunting and long; however, it also required each lesson to have an Anticipatory Set, also referred to as a Hook. The main idea was to relate the material to the students or grab their attention before introducing the material. In elementary school it was a simple matter to grab their attention, but secondary students are not as enthusiastic about learning at times.

Putting the students into the lesson is the strategy I've used to help them connect to the material. It may not be just at the beginning of the lesson, but teenagers are unique and at times challenging. If there is ever a way to have them involved in the material they are learning, then it is always my go-to strategy. I have done it for ELA as well as history. Novels lend themselves to role-playing. We read *The Lottery* by Shirley Jackson, and, after the story, I created a "lottery" to decide which student would have to present their answers to the class.

13

Grade What You Are Grading

This might sound like common sense, but it is amazing how many teachers do not actually grade what they tell students they are grading for. I have done this many times myself until this concept came to my attention.

How many times have you told a student in your class that you are grading content, but then take points off for spelling, length of answers, grammar, or colorful neatness? Here is the way it might go down:

A science teacher tells her students that they need to complete a paper on a topic, let's say it is an assigned mineral. They need to have:

♦ an image of the mineral;
♦ a description written;
♦ an explanation of where it can be found in the earth;
♦ a price on the mineral in today's market;
♦ a list of uses for the mineral.

Student A comes in with a beautifully colored piece of white paper, with neatly written information meeting all of the requirements.

Student B comes in with a poster – her mother makes letters with her Cricut machine, and there are plenty of sparkles and neatly arranged images. They have the information required, but it have a typo or two.

DOI: 10.4324/9781003370161-15

Student C has the project on a piece of white paper, written in pencil, and their writing is not neat at all. They have a poorly drawn image of the mineral and it is not colored. However, the information is correct, not lengthy, and meets the requirements without any spelling errors.

In my experience, Student B gets a high grade, then Student A, and Student C gets a low grade. The problem is" are you grading them on what you told them was required or are you grading them on their materials used? More importantly, are their materials ones they had access to?

I taught in a Title 1 district, and I made a decision years ago that I would never assign a project for which I could not provide the materials. I never asked a student to use poster paper if I did not have it to give out. I didn't ask students to print something unless I could offer them to print it in school. It is amazing just how many adults do not realize that not all students have equal access to supplies. I cannot remember the countless time I sent home crayons, markers, scissor, glue, or paper for a project or assignment.

We tell ourselves that Student A and Student B put more effort into the assignment, and we grade them accordingly; however, are you grading their effort or access to materials? Student C may have bad penmanship and maybe horrible artistic abilities; however, they met every requirement without any errors. Now any group of teachers would "judge" Student B to be the most impressive, but you are not grading the materials or the artwork … are you?

If you are grading for art, you need to ask if that is a standard in your curriculum. If you are grading for penmanship, you need to find the standard that relates *how* a student writes to their *knowledge* of the content. I have not seen an example of Albert Einstein's writing recently, but I would be willing to bet that his penmanship was not beautiful. Does that discount all of the realms of science and reality that he was able to understand and communicate so eloquently?

If you want students to present neat work, that needs not only to be on the rubric, but it also needs to be especially explained. Is that not using a pencil? Is that writing on lined paper or in a straight line? As you are describing exactly what "neatness," "appearance," or "effort" looks like on your rubric, you wonder what they have to do with a student demonstrating their understanding of the content.

Have you been grading students on how artistically inclined they are? Does the genius in your room get a pass for their penmanship, but the average student gets points off? Really, what are you grading and are you actually grading the content?

Without intention, many teachers end up grading parents, cars, and economics. Student B had parents who were not only home to help, but who also actually put their time and effort into the student's project. They had the time and the resources to go buy a posterboard. They had glue and sparkles in the house and a space for the student to assemble it all. I have taught those students. But I have also taught the other students. I have taught the students who do not have a pair of scissors in their home, never mind glitter or glue. The student whose parents worked two shifts and were not home to help them. The student who had to help raise their younger siblings and had barely any time to take a shower, never mind assemble a project or ask for a ride to the store. The student who cannot afford extra fancy supplies or the student whose parents use public transportation and the family that does not have a car or has to share one.

These are the students who routinely get lower marks because it appears that they didn't put effort into the project. And let's get real here – why do you need to feel like a student should be putting time and effort into your assignments? Will this prevent them from doing well on an exam? Will it keep them from learning? And just because you assume they did not put effort into the assignment does not mean that they did not. In fact, that student could be the one that has an impossibly difficult life outside of school and for them to even put it all together and get it completed was more effort than Student B, who has no challenges or responsibilities at home. Student C could've sacrificed being on time to get their sibling off of the bus or doing their wash at the laundromat just to have it completed for you. But, instead, we are so programmed to judge student effort by the way it appears.

We accept that a doctor has impossibly illegible writing, but we do not accept it from a student. We need to step back and look at what it is that we are grading. And, furthermore, what the purpose of the task serves.

Furthermore, do you take points off for spelling and grammar? Imagine that you assign an open-ended response to a question in social studies. The student answers the question in a way that demonstrates that they clearly have mastered the concept and has proven to you that they understand the material. Now let's say this student spells "there and their" incorrectly. Does that student lose points? In your social studies class, does a student need to spell correctly to explain to you the significance of the Silk Road?

It is helpful to correct the spelling so that they know they were using the word incorrectly or spelling something wrong and they can work to use it correctly in the future, but how does this impact their knowledge of the Han dynasty? I know that if I were a student, I would feel defeated if I confidently wrote about a topic that I have mastered only to find out that my "A became a B" because of my grammar. In fact, what does one have to do with the other? And is it realistic? In today's society, do our students need to know spelling? Will they be handwriting all of their work in college or in contract proposals? Yes, we should absolutely correct them so that they can write correctly, but punishing them for the mistakes seems very irrelevant and not aligned with content standards, unless it is ELA and you are grading spelling.

This is where I will be considered radical. As an ELA teacher, I did not take points off for spelling. Why? Because I wanted students to take risks in their writing and use words that they usually did not use. I would spell it correctly for them on their paper, but why would I punish a 13-year-old who used a word such as "colloquial" but sounded it out incorrectly? Instead, I would circle this great risk word and comment, "Wow! What a great word!" Then I would fix the spelling without taking off points. I wanted students to feel safe taking literary risks in their writing. I used it as an opportunity to learn, not an opportunity to be penalized.

The Takeaway

◆ Next time you give an assignment, ask yourself what your intention behind the assignment is. Unless you are teaching grammar, art, or spelling, maybe you should reconsider grading these exact skills. Meet the students where they are at. No one enjoys being corrected all of the time. Eventually, they might just not do anything out of embarrassment or fear. Pushing the grammar police into your assignments is not going to make or break a student's success. Drop the rope, it's a tug of war that is benefiting neither you nor the student. Teach, don't penalize.

14

Your Student Is Their Heart

Every district has their own unique relationship with the parents in the community or the community as a whole. I have found that stereotypes run deeply in urban education when it comes to reaching parents. I have heard comments about parents being "nowhere to be found," or "not interested in their child's education," more than once. Some say that Back to School Night (BTSN) is a good indicator of community and school relations. This is when those invested parents who truly care about their students show up to meet the teachers.

I call this a bunch of malarkey. As a parent myself, I have not been able to go to every BTSN, and it was not because I didn't care about my child's education. Life happens, and I have the luxury of working one job at a time during the school year. So if you are teaching in an area that is struggling socioeconomically, many parents, and even your students, have more than one job. When a parent is not easy to get in touch with, maybe it's because they, in fact, care so much about their children that they are picking up shifts or working more than one job to be able to provide for their children. Many Americans do not have the luxury of pulling in a salary good enough to provide for their family with one job anymore.

When my parents had my brothers and I, my father was able to get hired as a union laborer without a college degree, and his salary was often supplemented with side jobs. Even though

DOI: 10.4324/9781003370161-16

neither had a college degree, with his two jobs, my mom was able to stay home and raise the three of us until I entered elementary school. I know that when I went through a divorce and was a single mom for a spell, I had to walk away from a job I loved because I could not afford to live off of the salary the district negotiated. We are all put in situations where we need to make tough choices for our financial security. If that choice means that you cannot attend BTSN or parent conferences, or IEP meetings, it does not reflect the love a parent has for their child. These two things are not correlated and we, as educators, need to stop drawing an invisible line between the two.

Additionally, most teachers had a good experience in school, and, thus, they went into the field of education. This does not accurately reflect the experience of all adults. Think of one of your toughest students, and in them you may see a parent who still thinks of school as a horrible experience. To add insult to injury, our profession is known for a tendency to be condescending. A parent who is trying to get through conferences despite missing work or paying for a sitter does not need to have their grammar corrected or told that their child is going to amount to nothing. I avoid certain colleagues who think that they are superior and cannot help but to be condescending to others. I would dread them being the teacher of my child and sitting down without my vantage point of being an educator myself. If a colleague who has the same title and experience as I have can still make me feel inferior, imagine how these parents must feel.

Even if they are available to attend the conference times offered, and they are brave enough to enter an environment where they have always felt judged, there is a good chance that they will sit through another adult speaking critically about their child. My son has ADHD and a slew of other learning disabilities, including autism. When I sat before his teacher who was less than impressed with his progress in mastering his dyslexia and impulse control, I wanted to tell her that my son was going to quit her class. Obviously, I could not do such a thing, but even when I was very aware of the issues my child faced, I was still very agitated by her description of my child.

If you are a parent and a teacher, this may resonate. Most of my career I was not a mother, but I saw my brothers with their children, and it made the parents of my students seem more "human" in a way. I didn't judge my brother if he was unable to attend a school meeting. I certainly did not blame them for the academic challenges that my niece or nephew may have had. Yet, as educators, we seem to think that we are speaking about our students as just a name in our gradebook. When you speak to a parent or guardian of a student, imagine that you are speaking to your friend or family member who is doing their best to figure out the crazy role of parenting. None of us are trying to mess things up, and you need to always begin with humbleness and an open mind. Who are teachers to judge a mother, father, grandparent, or guardian without truly knowing them and their lot in life? No wonder parents do not want to meet with us.

This mentality needs to cross over to all communications with guardians. Phone calls and emails should never be anything but positive. This would enrage even the most admirable parent. If I have an issue with a student and I need to reach out to them through a phone call (the best option because a tone is hard to establish in writing) or an email, I always consider the child, not the student, whom I am about to speak about. Here is an example of what that conversation may look like:

Hi, this is Mrs. Matusz, XYZ's history teacher. How are you? So I want to let you know that I really enjoy having XYZ in my class this year. I see so much potential in them, especially when they contribute to our class discussions (or what an amazing artist they are, whatever their strength may be) and I just wanted to touch base because I do not want them going off track. XYZ hasn't been consistent with (HW, Behavior, etc.) and I really want to see them be successful this year. Is this something that you have noticed at home? Do you have suggestions for me to help them get back on track? Listen, you know XYZ better than anybody and I firmly believe that we are a team, and I would really like to see if we can work together to ensure their success in my class. I know that XYZ has a lot to offer, and they are a good kid, I think they may just need a little help or push getting back to the path they need to be on. If it is OK with you, I can keep you updated through emails or phone calls about their progress. I know it is really hard sometimes keeping track of school assignments, especially when they do not tell you, or you have more than one student at home. I know I do not keep on top of my son's work all of the time. It's hard being a working parent and managing our kids' education. So, please, let me know if you have any ideas that may help me with XYZ in my class, and if you could tell him that I called you and that we are on the same team trying to help him, that may go a long way.

Have a wonderful day, thank you so much for your time. I'm looking forward to helping XYZ reach his potential.

I have always had a positive reaction when I approach my conversations from a place of establishing a team with the parent. It's not their responsibility alone, just like it is not ours. It takes both in and out of school efforts to help a student really transform. If you have the mindset that your intention is to establish a support system for the student with their parent or guardian, then you will naturally speak to them in a kinder, more empathetic way. Many teachers tend to establish a tone of, "Your child is lazy, so what are YOU going to do about it?" Or, "I can only do so much for your child and I'm no longer going to try." These mindsets are completely inappropriate and such thinking needs to change on your end as the educator if you hope to make real progress with a parent's support at home.

Once a parent realizes that you *care* about their child, and that you see good in them, then you will have an ally at home who is willing to go to bat for you when the student begins blaming you for their choices. I honestly can say I do not know of a single parent who thinks their child is a horrible human being. Most parents would still love their child unconditionally even if they were to punch them in the face! A parent knows all of the factors that have molded their child into who they are. A teacher only knows a child for a very brief period of time and knows nothing beyond what they see manifesting in their classroom. Be kind. After all, you are speaking about a child.

Do not stop there! Call home to say something good. Especially those kids who you know are constantly getting bad calls home. Sure, they may deserve it, but no kid is all bad. Even in the darkest places, an educator has the beautiful ability to find the light in a child. That is what we do. This does not mean that you have to *like* a student, but, as an adult, we can find a positive attribute about a child.

I remember when I was able to recommend my students for honors classes, either from seventh into eighth grade, or from eighth grade into high school. Many students were expected to be recommended; however, if a student was not but was interested in a subject and I saw a spark in them, I always recommended them. They may not have written the best essays, but they were naturally interested and curious about the topic. This is the first step to success, the rest can follow if it is nurtured. As a result, I was able to recommend students who were not in any other honors programs. These were the best phone calls ever!

I did not have to call home, but I wanted to tell the parents personally because I knew that for some of these students, they were rarely recognized for positive behavior. I very clearly remember one mother crying when I told her that her son was going to be recommended for honors history. It went something like this:

Me: *"Hello, is this Mrs.____? Hi, I am XYZ's history teacher, Mrs. Matusz. I do not know if XYZ talked to you about our class, but they do really well in our class discussions, and I can see that they are naturally interested in history. I really enjoyed having them in my class this year (sometimes this is when the parent would seem taken aback or almost incredulous). Yea, so I wanted to let you know personally that I am recommending XYZ for the honors history class next year."*

Parent: *"What?! XYZ? Are you serious?"*

Me: *"Absolutely, XYZ has so much potential, and I'm so excited to give them this opportunity to excel."*

Parent: *"Oh my God, oh my God- (speaking to someone off-line) Hey! XYZ is going to be in honors next year!" Oh my God, I can't believe it, thank you, thank you so much. Oh God, wait until I tell his dad he is not going to believe it. I'm sorry, what was your name again?"*

These are the moments when I also tear up after I hang up the phone. To have told this mother that her child is *good enough*. That is all she wanted to hear. There are only so many times that a parent can be told that their child is *not good*. This one call validated how she felt about her own child, despite what she was hearing. The release of emotion made it clear just how long she had been holding out hope that someone else would see the same light that she knew her child had all along. These are the calls that I relish. These should be the calls we make.

The Takeaway

♦ I know that teaching is saddled with a bunch of jobs that are not in the actual description of the profession. In New Jersey, we have SGO's, PDP's, PLAP's, IEP's, 504's, data crunching, benchmarks, and a required number of exams and assignments. We have time to make only those phone calls that are urgent – if any at all. We have been burdened with a plate overflowing with things that detract from the real purpose of our profession. We are not statisticians, or copy editors, or counselors, or administrators.

Yet, we lose our own way when we have to choose between letting a parent know that their student had a great day or getting our grades into the gradebook. One of the worst things that has happened in education is the additional responsibilities that have oddly been placed at our feet. Let us teach, and we can move mountains. We can change lives, we can see every student, not just the struggling ones. It is a fight that we are all in as educators today. But it is a fight worth fighting. Whether we realize it or not, we are fighting not for our jobs but for the kids and their guardians. This new brand of teaching is also failing them, and we have to see them. Through all of the noise, we must always make the effort to see them. Even when we are pushed out to sea, we must fight the winds, the unfair expectations, the heavy load, we must find our way back to them. If we do not, then, what is it, exactly, that we do for a living?

15

Go to Them

Now that we have evaluated why some parents may not participate in school activities as much as we would like, how can we break down the boundary of the physical school building where we spend our hours and connect with the parents and the community?

As we often do so well, all we need to do is observe. I taught in a district that was beginning to collapse under the financial inability of homeowners to keep up with housing costs and in confronting the crime outside of the front doors. When I had my son, I would routinely go for walks with him around my neighborhood. I began to appreciate the differently painted front doors of the local houses. As a student of history, I appreciated the color of front doors whenever I was able to travel. It was something that I had always noticed and found pleasantly pleasing.

I was on one of these routine walks with my son when I had an epiphany. I decided to paint my front door. So I took inventory of the neighbors' doors and finally arrived at a color that I thought would look great – a shade of yellow that I later came to resent. However, it was while painting over the white with this pop of color that I had the more important epiphany: I could do this downtown in my district.

Now due to my open-minded administrators and a community coalition, I was able to pitch my idea and get the go-ahead to proceed. I lived about 35 minutes away from the district that

DOI: 10.4324/9781003370161-17

I taught in, so I needed to spread the word about my new volunteer service in whatever way I could. First, I built a website called The Front Door Project. Within the site was an app that allowed residents to schedule a time on Saturday or Sunday to have me arrive to paint their front door with a fresh coat of paint.

My motto was that I had the time and a lot of random paint colors in my garage thanks to my inability not to apply a pop of color to every room in my house, regrettably. Yet, I wanted more options for the residents to choose from. So I was referred to a local hardware store in the district. I stopped by and spoke to the owner, explained my outreach program, and he agreed to donate some paint. I had to do more than throw on a fresh coat of paint for these families. I understood that there was a more serious need than "cleaning up" the area. So I went over to the local LOWES store and asked to speak to the manager.

After explaining my proposal, he agreed to donate to the cause. This wonderful young man gave me about 20 brand-new front door locks and knobs. Finally, the project took shape, and I was ready for the last step. I have always loved speaking to people, especially about my passions. So through the community coalition I was put in contact with a local news channel. I dressed in my best casual, yet professional teacher attire and arrived at the studio ready to talk. The man in charge – his name was Jim – was generous enough to give me a 30-minute interview. We sat at a table, and he asked me questions and I answered them. The interview aired on both the local TV station and the radio. I left the studio feeling high from the experience.

The project culminated in only about five doors being repainted and fixed. The first weekend, I asked other teachers to get involved. After that, it was just me. My grand idea was that getting into the community would help bridge the connection between the teachers and the parents. If the parents did not have the time or the desire to come to my classroom, then I would go to them while offering a much-needed service for free. I jokingly told the journalist who interviewed me that I needed to be inside the front door at some point in order to paint it. If a parent did not want to talk to me, that was fine, but I could talk to a lamp post, so, I was fairly confident that we would end up exchanging at least some words. Once they get me in that door, I will talk their ear off. I did just that most of the time.

If this outreach program had hit its stride to become what I had hoped it would, it would have resulted in both local police and teachers painting front doors – two professionals in the community who seemed the most out of touch with the residents. I envisioned administrators and officers, sleeves rolled up and out of their work clothes, getting messy and putting in the effort to help beautify the community. I felt that there were not enough opportunities for parents to see us as fellow parents, workers, and human beings. A suit and a uniform have a way of placing an unspoken social caste upon those around them. I wanted these families, and their students, to see the human beneath the work clothes. It is a lot harder to think someone is your foe if you watch them helping others whom you care about.

The last door that I painted had snuck up on me. The resident had scheduled the appointment through the website, and I had not noticed. I arrived with a bunch of paint cans to choose from, big rolls of paper, painting tape, brushes, and pans ready to complete the job. I had learned early on that many of the doors required prep before they could be painted. I spent a decent amount of time scrapping the previous color paint chips from the door. Another thing that I had not considered was the number of coats that it would take to completely cover the door. These were the things that probably prevented my concept from really taking off.

On this specific occasion, I was on Third Street by 8:30 am with a cup of coffee, podcasts at the ready, and a lot of materials to unload. After introducing myself and helping the owner of the house decide on a color of paint, I set out to enjoy the morning painting the door. The resident was very gracious but not necessarily in the mood to chat beyond the first 20 minutes. She had things to do, as did I, so I put on my podcast and began chipping off the old black paint from the door. I remember the sun shining, and it was a promising beginning to a spring day. The streets were quiet so early in the morning, and I was away from my baby boy enjoying the stillness of the new day. A car drove by and then turned around. This community was no stranger to gang activity, and, for a moment, I wondered what someone would have against me or the sweet homeowner.

The passenger door opened and my former student, Di'jana, hopped out of the car and then it sped off in the original direction it was going. To say that I was surprised would be an understatement. It turned out that she saw me as she was driving by and had asked the driver to turn around and drop her off. Not a move I would expect from a 15-year-old at 9 am on a Saturday. I welcomed the company, and I would find out later after she had passed in a tragic car accident that she had recorded much of our morning that day.

The door was originally painted black, and the homeowner had chosen a deep red, the color I had painted my own door on my second attempt. The color was dark, but not dark enough. After the first coat, it was clear that there would need to be a second and maybe even a third coat to do the job right. Diij (as they called her) and I cleaned up some supplies and told the owner that we would step out and be back for the second coat.

I was starving, so with her grandma's permission, I drove us to WaWa to get some sandwiches. I grabbed myself a coffee as well, but I knew that Starbucks was a trendy treat and that Diij probably did not often go there. We joked around while in line to order, and she was hesitant to allow me to buy her anything. I made her order the works, and we sat for a few minutes at a high table inside the café. It was the expected awkward former student-teacher conversation. As always, I had asked her how school was going. She responded with the fleeting teenage answer that only partly addressed my concerns. She seemed less interested in conversation than she was in roasting me.

Di'jana had a great sense of humor, and it was easy to go back and forth when she launched the first joke at my expense. I always won, but I would let her banter for a while before shutting it down. In the car back to the house, she thought my rap music was hilariously outdated and not suited to what she assumed that I had listened to. Every time I looked in her direction when she called my name, she had her camera up and I just shook my head. This was a time when social media only consisted of Facebook and SnapChat had just appeared on the horizon – much simpler times. Still, I told her that she couldn't share her directorial debuts with any students. I had kept my personal life separate from my job and wanted it to stay that way.

Fast forward six years, and when her sister finally acquired her phone from the car wreck, she shared these videos with me. It is truly amazing how we can take for granted the appreciation and even admiration that students can have for us. It was so clear in all the videos from that morning that Diij was in awe of her eighth grade history teacher, and I hadn't realized it in the moment, nor the many moments after. They are painful to watch now; I wish I had allowed myself to really talk to her, make sure that she was OK. Both she and I resorted to humor in a serious or awkward situation, and it was never more evident than on those short video clips. Though when the video would end on a frame of her face, I cannot believe I had never understood just how much she seemed to care for me. Whenever I find myself feeling sad about her loss, I just roast her in my mind, and I swear I can still hear her comebacks – this time I let her win.

Once we arrived back to apply the second coat of red paint, it was already 11:30 am and the morning grew into an even more gorgeous day. When it was very apparent that a third coat of red paint would be necessary to complete the job, the homeowner finally told me to go home.

"Go home and enjoy the day with your son," she said, having already learned about my life through small talk. I tried to refuse, but it seemed that she was ready to enjoy not having a teacher in her house any longer, and so I left. Di'jana and I packed up the car and I drove her back home to her grandma's house. Right before she got out of the car, I snatched my Yankees hat off of her head before she could steal it from me. It was a playful gesture, but I wish I had let her keep it.

Not every effort to reach out beyond the school building needs to be so extravagant and time consuming. After I ended up leaving to teach in a new district, I still kept in touch with local community members. I felt like I had to abandon my kids in one of those hard choices that parents have to make for financial stability. More than any other district, these students had my heart. Now I am able to help the city in partnership with an incredible grassroots outreach program. I have come to know and admire the local parents and employees who make up this fantastic organization. Every time I see a post of theirs on social media, I smile. I know these adults are taking care of "my kids" and I feel less guilty.

Just a little ambition can go a long way. You never know an answer unless you ask. If you are volunteering time or supplies, the answer is almost always a yes. I would often stay after school with students who had to get work completed and, once they got home, they felt as if they didn't have the time or space to do so. I also once organized a health and fitness group. I had my students, and once even my amazing vice principal, running stairs and doing sprints, wall-sits, and planks twice a week. Many of the kids just wanted to have fun, but letting them run around the halls with my supervision seemed like they were breaking the rules in a safe way. I never saw so many smiles while sprinting.

I am aware of the work overload that we face as teachers. I understand the need to go home to your family. Nevertheless, if you could find a way to connect with your students outside of the classroom, it makes a difference. Just as the parents may see us as stuffy, arrogant teachers, students have a hard time envisioning the human being who we are outside of the context of the classroom. If your district has any stipends for clubs, poll your kids to see what they are interested in. Find a way for them to meet the person that you are when you are not putting out fires in your class or pushing through a lesson.

The Takeaways

♦ Humility works inside the class, but outside the class students also see your dedication to them and the time that you consider them worthy of. It also opens up the opportunity for other students whom you may not teach to get to know you. Nothing is more influential for a teenager than the opinion of their peers. If their friends think you're cool, then you have more than just good classroom management tools, you have "cred." Credibility, my friend, is the highest form of currency in the secondary years. For some students, that credibility may come from the fact that you also play video games or that you watched the game last night. Maybe they find out you play an instrument or any other nugget of information about you that class schedules do not always allow them to learn about you. After school time slows down, this is when those connections are figured out for your students.

◆ Find your local reporters for publicity when you organize events. Administrators are always on board for positive news about their schools, and contacting the local media also reaches parents who may not read the school newsletter or class calendars.

16

If You're Not a Little Weird, You're Not Normal

In case you have not yet figured out the overarching theme of my stories, it is that being a bit odd or quirky, as some may call it, is what makes you the interesting teacher. Think back to any movie or TV show that portrayed a teacher as good or "cool," I guarantee you that teacher was a bit out of the box.

Whether it's your passion for your content, your ability to make everything into a pun, your bad dad jokes, or your eclectic neckwear collection, the students notice this about you. All of these things require a lot of confidence. Although we went into a career of teaching, not all teachers are confident beyond standing in front of their students.

I had a Spanish teacher in high school who absolutely adored Tom Selleck. She had a life-size cardboard image of him, and she always worked him into her lessons, "Let's conjugate the verb to say that Thomas Selleck is hungry." This teacher was always enthusiastic, over the top, and she made Spanish fun. Not only did she make it fun, but I also excelled in her class. I will always remember her fondly, as I can still remember where the room was located in my school, what she looked like, and how little I knew about Tom Selleck!

This is no different from another superb teacher I had for a class named Man's Inhumanities to Mankind. Now if you are wondering how a teacher made such a sobering class fun, you'd

DOI: 10.4324/9781003370161-18

be right to be scrupulous. Mr. Cuff did not make the class fun; the content was absolutely daunting and very heavy for a tenth grader. However, his passion for the topic and his infinite knowledge in any direction a tangent could go was unlike any other. I still remember his sweater vests, dark dress pants, and dress shoes. When learning about the intimidating SS officers during World War II, he would stand at attention and the sound of the soles of his shoes on the laminate flooring would send a chill down my spine. The work was intense, a very rigorous class indeed, although I couldn't wait to take it even as a mere sophomore because my older brother had taken it many years before and I remembered him telling me all about his class.

This teacher knew an immense amount of history, yet he could stir any teenager's emotions by playing "The Sound of Silence" by Simon and Garfunkle, in relation to a poem about the Holocaust. Even before the concept of multiple intelligences, many great teachers were incorporating not just text, but also movie clips, music, and art. I had an English teacher my senior year who was also very odd but did a brilliant job teaching us Shakespeare through, of all bands, Pink Floyd. To this day, if I hear "Comfortably Numb" I think of *King Lear*.

I think that teachers today have a tendency to believe that we are hip to the educational revolution by having a class playlist or dressing up for a specific lesson. Yet, many great teachers laid this foundation many decades ago. It is amazing that we have come full circle. To me, it's simple: forget all the latest acronyms, Pinterest boards, and bloggers. It's passion, knowledge, and the confidence to be a little weird that have always been the ingredients that make up an amazing teacher. I firmly believe that all "good" teachers know what and how to teach their material. Just humanize the lesson, think about what you would want to do for the lesson if you were a student in your class. Not every lesson is a high-energy performance. We are actors, but not for the screen or the stage; rather, we go to our theater every day intending to act passionate and curious enough about what we need to teach in order to convince our students to give us a chance to teach them.

There is no formula for being a bit odd; however, many of us have certainly mastered it. I have found that other than my inability to be humiliated, I naturally embrace the weirdness that I bring to the lessons. The other day, I had a student find a little water beetle on my class floor. Instead of them crushing it, I picked it up. I temporarily placed it in a tiny (desktop size) recycling bin with a connected lid, a great dollar store find. The next class came in and I did not have time to run him either outside or to the science teacher.

I was mid-lesson when there was a lethargic silence in response to the question I had just posed to the class. So, without thinking, I picked up this tiny trash can, opened the lid, and asked out loud, "What do you think Harry?" As you might imagine, my students did think this was odd, but they had already grown accustomed to my oddness (I really overachieve in this arena), so it was not something they asked for an explanation about. In fact, we rolled into the next part of the lesson. I was aware that I must seem very strange for them not to even question my conferring with Harry, but I kept moving. Once another opportunity presented itself, I once again asked Harry his opinion. Eventually, I had to explain that I was conversing with my new "co-teacher." Still, they simply shrugged as if that were a good enough explanation for my strange behavior.

By the third time, students began to ask me what (I corrected them that they should say who) was in the container. I replied very matter of factly that it was, indeed, Harry my new co-teacher. Once again, I kept the lesson moving and no longer referred to Harry – until the very last few minutes of class. Of course, a curious student came up to inquire as we were waiting to be dismissed, so I dumped the beetle out onto my hand and the student shrieked! I give all the credit to my seven-year-old son, who handles bugs and all things "natural" in the most respectful manner. So this tiny beetle did not freak me out in the least bit. But it was definitely not a group favorite when I offered him to passing students on their way to the bus. I handed it to my colleague right across the hall for his science class, and it was over, but not until I had some fun with the tiny visitor.

I had a colleague who once made a globe into his class bathroom pass. Try looking cool in the halls carrying a globe. It wasn't a chic small globe you'd find in a home decor store; this was an old-school huge history classroom globe. This was a district with many hallway altercations, but never once did the globe become an issue. It was always brought to the restroom and returned. I wondered if this also cut down on the number of students who thought about wandering the halls during his class. Pretty ingenious; everyone knew that the students with the globe belonged in his history class.

One day I was teaching a class that was my last class of the day. This class was smaller, and so it had quickly acquired a family-like atmosphere early in the year. I had a student who was wonderful at dead-pan humor. This student had realized that it was the 22nd day of the 2nd month in the year 2022 – 2/22/22. He asked if we could have two minutes of silence at 2:22, which was about mid-class. I had to say yes, it was a no-brainer for me! I will always remember standing in silence for those 120 seconds with those kiddos. What a mindful moment. So-called experts and educational coaches fly in from all over the country to tell teachers about whatever new trending techniques they should be using in their classrooms. I think I should suggest this strategy for mindfulness next time I get a chance to speak to an expert.

The Takeaway

♦ There is a popular movie that recently came out called *Yes Day*. The storyline is that two parents say "yes" to every one of their children's requests. This is not an effective way to manage a classroom; however, some things are not going to make or break a lesson and is a moment that is teachable or at least memorable. The two minutes that my class and I sat in silence did not ruin my lesson. It did, however, make the students super excited and they told the story over and over. Sometimes maybe we should challenge ourselves to go off-script for just a short spell. If you've been teaching for more than a year, you already realize that the sooner you let go of the concept that you are going to execute your lesson exactly as planned, the easier teaching will be.

17

Thrift Life Forever

One of the strange things about being a secondary education teacher is that often the students will begin to mimic your behaviors if you are "lucky" enough to get the "cool teacher" label. In my experience, being cool is the teenager translation for authentic, honest, good human. Though, in this unique position, you could make the decision to do something that effects positive change.

When I was a young girl, my family never seemed underprivileged, and I don't remember ever wanting for anything. We were a typical family of five, living in a three-bedroom ranch house, my two older brothers shared a room, and I had the third to myself. Days were spent in the woods behind our house, evenings in front of the TV watching the lineup on TBS: *Family Matters, Full House,* and *The Fresh Prince of Bel-Air.* My mother always had dinner on the table around 5:30, and even as my brothers got old enough to drive off to a friend's house, they always seemed to sneak home right on time for dinner before going back out.

My father was a union pipefitter, a laborious career often spent outside at refineries in Newark, NJ, or at power plants like Oyster Creek. Our dinner table conversation was always the same. I am not sure how they managed it, but they had us engaged every dinner in lively conversation. Many nights it was the battle of wits – who was clever enough to refer back to that funny joke

DOI: 10.4324/9781003370161-19

when a new story was told. "Nobody likes a wise guy," I remember my father saying despite delivering all the best humor at the table. Our mandatory glasses of bright, white whole milk stood watch over the colorful plates – always containing a meat, a carbohydrate, and a vegetable, and all homemade by my mother who grew up too fast, having to cook and care for siblings.

Each night I would fall asleep to the humming noise of my humidifier or, my favorite, the cathedral of crickets, tree frogs, and cicadas outside my window. To this day, if I am ever directed to imagine that I am in my happy place, I can envision it like it was just yesterday. My mom in her bedroom watching *Wheel of Fortune* or *Little House on the Prairie* after she made the official nightly announcement, "kitchen closed," turning off the switch and heading down the hall. This was the time she had earned. Working, cooking, cleaning – now, as a mother myself, I understand just how necessary that time to herself was.

My brothers would be home, either one on the couch in the living room or both in their room – on their personal house line or playing a Sega video game. I am with my dad in the living room. We would sit on a wooden rocking chair that he pulled in front of the TV. The rhythmic rocking and the sound of Bobby Murcer calling the Yankees game was always a winning combination. The front door was open, and the screen door allowed in a brief humid breeze, damp from the summer rain. The symphony of crickets kept beat, singing with the rocker as I drifted into a dream.

Sometimes it is not until we are an adult that we can see from a different perspective the things that we held to be perfect for so long. My father was laid off often – the economy had yet to reflect Clinton's policies, he'd say. Thus, he was out of work at the union, and that meant my parents had to figure out how to keep the kids from realizing that we may be going without some things. They did a heck of a job because, as I said, I never wanted for a thing.

In reality, there were some struggles. Most went unnoticed by my younger self. It was not until about the third grade that I felt like I may have been "out of place" in a way. My mother took pride in dressing my brothers and I for school, and now I realize how tough it must've been with three growing children.

My brothers had many male cousins who would hand down clothes, or they would even share some between themselves. I had only one female cousin around my age, and she was still six years older than I and a completely different size.

It was Halloween, maybe Kindergarten or first grade, and we were marching through the classes in our costumes for the sake of entertaining the older kids in the school. I remember being so self-conscious about my costume. It was like a clown, but it had these huge furry balls down the center as buttons. I remember holding those furry pompoms to hide them from the view of the cooler, older kids. However, even this slick move would not prove to be good enough to make me feel more comfortable. I was wearing a leotard, the type found in a dance recital. No bottoms, just the outline of my underwear obviously peeking through my opaque white tights. The outfit was completed with Velcro sneakers and ankle socks.

Every kid gets a little embarrassed by their outfits at times. But then there was the third- grade picture day outfit that I was wearing when I met my best friend. Cute paisley cotton dress, lace-trimmed collar of the white long-sleeved button-down shirt beneath it, huge half-up hair style with an even more offensively large purple acrylic bow. My mother had decided to support her friend's new side hobby with a moment that would be forever captured in time.

None of this was really abnormal for me, but the thick, iridescent purple tights and glittered jazz shoes were. My cousin happened to be an alien in her dance recital a few years previous, and so these became staples of my wardrobe my third-grade year. I think people began assuming I had a very loud style, but, in reality, I don't remember much choice. Many leotards spanned across my childhood. Though they were in style, mine were odd, pea-green, with a pink stripe diagonally running down my non-existent chest. I remember climbing the rope in gym class in fifth grade and being so proud that I had made it all the way to the ceiling only to be made fun of when I got back down to Earth because I had sweat stains running through the armpits of my tight, thick, long-sleeved green gymnastic leotard. I was mortified and had no idea how much my clothes would start to betray my confidence.

I was at a roller rink birthday party; it was about fourth or fifth grade. I still remember getting ready for the party. These parties were so fun because you got dropped off by your parents and then there was a great sense of independence as you rolled around the rink with your friends, laughing and also trying to look steady on your feet. I had spent a very long time putting my hair into a high ponytail with a gold cone clip. Imagine a typical "I love Jennie" hairstyle. My hair was thick and not well maintained, but I brushed through all of the knots to make it long enough to fit into the triangle atop my head. So far, so good, I thought. Next, the outfit. I had picked a pair of jeans, white-washed, tapered at the bottom, ruffled flower-printed waistband. Then I put on a cropped lime green t-shirt with shoulder-pads and huge black round buttons, five of them going down the middle.

Unlike my clown costume, these buttons were flat, with what felt like a plastic button beneath the black fabric that covered it. The only issue was that this shirt had one button that was "missing" the cover. The outside was covered in black fabric, but the inside circle was brown cardboard. I quickly color the center of the button with a black Sharpie marker. It wasn't perfect, but it was not as obvious as it had been.

All my ten-year-old confidence was out on show as I crossed my feet over one another taking the corners of the rink to Madonna. I was having a blast, just as I knew I would. After the pizza that tasted (and looked) like cardboard, and the poorly fla-vored ice cone, my friends and I went back out for our last laps around the rink. It was then that a girl whom I did not recognize, about my age or even a bit older, approached me. I am not sure if my memory is correct, but I believe we were both standing in the middle of the rink, avoiding collision with the skaters. She had a friend with her, and she said to her friend, not so much to me, "Oh my God! It is my shirt! Where did you get my shirt?" I had no idea what she was referring to. I had never really paid much attention to where my clothes had come from, but that blissful ignorance was about to end. I knew that I never had the same clothes that my friends had. Or maybe, even better put, my friends never had the same clothes that I wore.

"That's my shirt, you're wearing my shirt!" We both looked at my shirt, both amazed. For sure she was mistaken, I thought. "Yea, that's mine, the button came off, so I got rid of it." At this moment I had a brief pause of hope since my buttons were all on. "Look! There, did you color it in with a Sharpie?" The girls began to laugh, and I pushed off on my skates and into the dark corners of the rink.

As an adult, I look back and remember the comments girls made to me, "What happened to you? You used to dress so weird and now you dress cool?"

My dad had been elected business agent for his local and it had changed our lives. He went from pumping gas and being a golf catty during his days off to having a company car and wearing a suit instead of something from Carhartt. This was sixth grade for me, and, to my recollection, the first time that I went school shopping to pick out clothes. I still remember the store that I went to in the mall that had my small size. I remember my picture day, as I was so excited to wear my zipper-up plaid t-shirt and necklace that my mom had let me pick out.

In reality, the paper we used at the Can Can Sales were food stamps, and the eclectic wardrobe I wore were all handouts, from family, Goodwill, or whatever my mom could get for me. Even as I grew up and my father had a steady, lucrative job, I was always more aware of what I was wearing. However, I had been blessed with a sense of confidence that I should not have carried. The idea of wearing the "right labels" or having the "right shoes" never really bothered me. As my father once told me, "Don't ever be a slave to fashion, Pam. Just wear what you want to wear." And so I did and still do to this day. That little girl on the roller rink had to find a level of confidence that was almost unattainable for such a young kid. I stayed for the rest of the party that day and I acted as if nothing had happened. The girl and her friend would continue to make rude remarks to me, but I was too busy working on my crossover skills to hear them, or at least that's what I told myself. Both then and now.

So here I am, the girl with all the weird leotards, and my middle school students often look up to me. For me, this journey seems unlikely, but, nevertheless, they seem to continue to believe that I am worthy of their admiration. I had long since stopped thinking about that little girl in the green cropped shirt and had made many more important memories by the time I was in my early thirties. I am teaching sixth grade social studies in a new district after a dramatic move from my previous home district of seven years. At this time in my life, I had inherited teenage step kids, and I think the constant obsession with clothing labels and fitting the fad had really begun to sink into my unconscious mind.

I had noticed a few of my students scoffing at a pair of shoes that another student was wearing. In this district, brand "A" was cool, but brand "B" was not. I noticed that all of these unspoken rules changed from school to school and were purely the creation of the students themselves – like a self-imposed uniform policy, except that students got bullied rather than disciplined for an infraction of the code. I did not want to show up to teach in a trending brand that my students were wearing. I just felt as if I were immediately putting myself in a category with the "popular" or "wealthy" kids. Let's face it – no educator is making the big bucks to be sporting Kanye Yeezy sneakers anyway!

I had heard about a teacher making a statement by wearing the same outfit each day. I was not sure what her motivation was or how long she had worn it, but I did know the only thing stopping me from doing the same thing was my sense of humility. If the only factor in a decision is bravery, I am usually always in. So I chose a very bright cotton maxi dress that I had worn only once before. The colors and patterns were beautiful, but, more importantly, they were not subtle in the least. My intention was to make it very obvious that I was wearing the same exact dress each and every day.

When I first embarked on this adventure, I was not sure how long I would wear the same outfit. Therefore, I have some helpful hints should you want to also be a beacon for bullied students.

1. Think layers. I chose a cotton dress that I could put a cardigan over or leggings under. I wore the same shoes for the most part. However, at least here in New Jersey, the wise teacher always plans for adding or removing layers throughout the day.

2. I chose a colorful patterned dress in case I stained it during my streak wearing the same item. Maybe it would be less obvious if it wasn't all one solid color.
3. Consider the fabric and the effect that washing on drying will have on it. My dress shrunk so much that I had to cut it into a shirt!
4. Make sure you are comfortable but don't choose jeans. Jeans are considered a "dress down" day in many districts where I teach. I didn't want to seem like I was using the opportunity to wear jeans to work every day.
5. In the United States, October is anti-bullying month or bullying-prevention month. Therefore, to have a consistent message and a clear deadline, I now do this during the entire month of October. If the last day, Halloween, is a school day, I usually break the streak by dressing like "someone who changes their outfit." It is a creative way to end it, and it also gives you an exit.

Each day we would keep count of how many days it had been that I wore the same outfit. I'd have a student write it on the board to keep it updated. As I had said, when I first did this, I didn't have a specific timeline set. I ended up wearing the same dress for six weeks. By the time June had rolled around, I had already cut my dress to make it a shirt because it had shrunk a decent amount. It was so short that I had to wear leggings under it, but we had no air conditioning in our classrooms, and I was on the second floor. Needless to say, cutting it into a shirt was clutch. Once the six weeks were over, I cut it into a strip and wore it tied around my hair, like Rosie the Riveter. On the last day of school, students were lobbying for my headband to keep as a memento from the year (I was leaving the district and they would never see me again).

This became the ultimate same-day-outfit send off. I cut the fabric into small pieces, enough for my 75 students. I called each student up and gave them a piece one by one. I have since had students reach out to me through email years later and let me know that they still have that piece of my dress as a reminder not to try to fit in all the time.

The Takeaways

◆ If you decide to do this, make sure your administration is made aware of the social stance you are taking in solidarity with the students who are bullied. I have found that this cause is something districts like to publicize. It's also more meaningful if the entire school is aware of your action. I would tell the roller rink story over the morning announcements on October 1st to explain the purpose of my actions and to relay the message very clearly that bullies are not cool.

If this gets you too much attention, but you still like the concept, I also practice a very strategic thrifting style. On the first few days of school, I make sure I wear clothes that I bought from my local thrift shop. It seems that early in the year, the female students can be super kind and complimentary. So anytime that I get a compliment on a dress or shirt, I tell them very loudly, "Thanks! It was $2 at Goodwill." Another thing I do to show solidarity with the students whose parents cannot afford the new and cool brands, I never wear "branded" clothes. I buy my shoes at Burlington or Ross. I never shop at the mall.

◆ I once found out that these shoes, Yeezy sneakers, were averaging about $600 to $800 per pair. I looked them up and was amazed. My students loved watching me flabbergasted as I scrolled down the page and reacted to the prices of these shoes! Yes, I did it in class. It came up in a discussion that we had been having about an article that we read. A no brand shoe store paid to rent a location on Rodeo Drive in Beverly Hills, CA, and created a fake designer. They then stocked the store with their own no brand shoes and paid models and actors as the employees. The experiment went so far as inviting some local influencers to attend the new location opening.

Wouldn't you know, people were picking up these shoes and making comments about the quality, the design, and the pure genius of this up-and-coming designer. Some customers actually paid $300 to buy a pair, when, in reality, they sold for less than $20! I like to read this as a non-fiction passage because it sets the stage for kids to open up about labels, and the pressure of fitting in.

◆ That is some of the thinking behind teaching secondary students. We need to read certain genres and cover certain skills. However, sometimes we can not only look for materials that fit the standards but also examine themes that are relevant to the generation we teach. Some texts are classic and can stand the test of time. Others, if allowed, should be updated and adopted to reflect the current issues that our students face. As a teacher of ancient history for many years, I have perfected the art of finding ways to make "unrelatable topics" relevant to contemporary generations. In the end, we are all stories.

III

Teaching the Toughest Kids

18

In School Suspension Sucks

Many secondary schools have an in-school suspension (ISS) policy. Often this is the "punishment" for students whose behavior is too outrageous for detention but not bad enough to warrant expulsion. The concept is that they are restricted to a room for the day to complete work inside the school. They report to school, but they are not allowed to circulate in the "general population" and are watched over by the teacher in charge. There is often no talking allowed and they sit mostly in silence as the punishment for their behavior.

I was an ISS teacher for two years, and when it was my time on the rotation, I looked forward to it because I would have six hours of silence. I would get through two books in a week, and one time I even hand-made wedding invitations while shoved into the "closet" of the IMC, which was where this school's ISS room was located.

After many years of teaching, I began to resent ISS. I went out of my way to avoid having a student leave my room and put a lot of effort into keeping them in class. Other teachers may have written up a student and it resulted in ISS. I don't shame those teachers for doing so. I understand that, after a while, it seems that there is no other option. However, because a teacher in another class wrote up my student, they would miss MY class also. These were the kids who were the most challenging, and often they were the most challenging because they struggled with school in

DOI: 10.4324/9781003370161-21

general. I still maintain that a 14-year-old boy would rather get thrown out of class than admit that they cannot read.

This resulted in my lowest level students missing the most days of instruction. Not because I kicked them out, but because they acted up in another class. They may have been great in my class, but it did not matter. They were in the ISS room all day long. I would have to send them work, and so I made a habit of walking it down to them so I could have a conversation with them about why they were there. I would do my best to explain the assignment to them, but it more often than not came back blank in my office mailbox the next morning.

Some ISS teachers were very strict and towed the line. They checked the work students were assigned and kept the peace. Others just had ISS for one period during their teaching schedule and, sadly, the result was a revolving door of teachers every period of the day. There was no stability, no open line of communication, and, as you might expect, the students exploited it. I would frequently walk into a room when delivering my assignments to a student and encounter chaos. Chewing gum, talking, not doing a lick of work – the students were running the room. Even in the best-case scenario, ISS teachers could not physically force the hand of a student who refused to do work or teach them the lessons that they were missing.

Nonetheless, ISS was not a deterrent to these kids. In fact, some kids saw it as a way to sleep away the school day rather than have to complete work in class. I began to see it as a flaw in the system. I met with my vice principal (VP), who was very open to input from teachers. I found that at this district where I taught for seven years, the administrators had an "open-door" policy and were always willing to give a green light to staff ideas. This made all the difference in the world. Because of their willingness to collaborate, I was able to do things in this school that were above and beyond teaching in the classroom. I have never felt as supported in any other district, and, therefore, I have never been able to implement such ideas elsewhere. In most districts the administrators will send you to another person along the chain of command to get a green light for your proposal. Even if it was not a budget issue, and you were offering the time for free, there was an immense amount of red tape to navigate.

I was so fortunate to land in this particular district for my first tenured position. The building-level administration policy was always, "why not?" instead of "contact this person." As a result, teachers were able to flourish in the areas they excelled in outside of their classrooms. My specialty has always been to connect to the tough kids. I saw the ISS policy as a detriment both to the students and to the goal of education in general. So I sat down in the office of my vice principal and pitched an idea.

I had first period prep, which means that after my homeroom, or advisory, I was "off" until the second class of the day. Anything that a teacher does during their prep is built into their contract, and, if you are forced to cover a class or assume a duty, you had to be compensated per the NJEA. I knew this was my only obstacle to pitching my new idea, so I chose to volunteer my prep and take on a duty for free.

Each Monday, I would go to the VP's office and collect the students who were slotted for ISS that day. At the discretion of the VP, considering the "offense" that landed students in ISS along with approval given by a parent over the phone, I would take supervision of these students for as many Mondays as assigned by the VP to "work" off their ISS time. Each Monday I collected as many eighth graders as were waiting for me, and we began by putting on latex gloves. I would lead them to the cafeteria, where we filled buckets with warm water and took the Magic Eraser sponges supplied by my enthusiastic VP and we got to work.

We cleaned lockers, we cleaned the walls, and often, if it was nice weather, we would pick up trash on campus. I had about 40 minutes with these students and that was all the time I needed. You see, many of the students I was assigned were not the students that I taught. Or, as I affectionately refer to them, "not my kids." The key was that I would scrub the school and pick up trash right alongside them. I would ask them why they were assigned ISS and we would get to know one another. I was able to build a rapport with these students, and, after our 40 minutes were up, I'd go back to teaching and they went about their normal schedule.

Over time, I had frequent flyers, or kids that were assigned several weeks of "work" for their write up. When they saw me in the hallways they would shout, "Matusz!" It was nice to cross over to other "teaching teams" as we referred to them. With about 400 eighth graders, there were three teachers for every subject. So I only taught a third of the eighth graders in my school. This meant that I had no contact with two-thirds of the eighth graders. This may seem irrelevant, but when you teach in a "tough" school, your credibility is the most important tool that you have as a teacher.

You see, if I saw a student fighting or misbehaving in the halls, it helped that they knew me or knew *of* me. It is amazing how a teacher's "popularity" earned a level of respect that would influence the way a student interacted with me. Most teachers in this school had figured this out, and most of us had a reputation not because we let them get away with bad behavior or we tried being their "friends" but because our actions and our words made it clear to them that we cared about them and respected them.

For the duration of my time teaching at this school, I volunteered my prep period to keep students out of ISS. They didn't miss their education, and parents were happy to have them "work" off their discipline rather than have them sit in a room all day and sleep. Parents often thanked the VP for this offer and saw it as more productive and as a more effective deterrent. In fact, the VP took my idea even further and assigned some students to work after school with the custodians instead of mandating traditional discipline alternatives. If schools are charged with the task of educating students, then why would we enforce a punishment for behavior that keeps them out of the classroom and deprives them of their education? There must be better ways to handle discipline, and we must do better as educators and leaders of education.

Teachers who do not find a balance often assume that the teachers who are popular with students must be so because they are easy on them in class or look the other way when they misbehave. This could not be further from the truth in my experience. Just yesterday, I had a heart to heart with a student and told him that he was pushing away help because of his pride, and that he needed to drop the tough-guy act if he wanted to pass seventh grade. I probably got more "real" with him than any of his teachers. I referred to a family member about whom he often spoke to me, and I told him that he was on the same path if he didn't stop acting like a fool.

We stood in silence for a moment, and I asked him this question: when was the last time you got a hug? He looked shocked, and, other than at his grandma's birthday the week prior, he could not remember. These are the tough conversations that "cool" teachers have. In complete contrast with our colleagues' stereotype of us, we don't let kids get away with things, we treat them like they are our own. Like many of my colleagues over the years, we have understood that our compassion for and investment in our students is what makes us "cool." A teenager can smell a contrived conversation a mile away. Teachers who get flustered when challenged by a student are like chump in the water. Compassion cannot be faked around a teenager, and compassion is what makes a teacher extraordinary. The moment that a teacher shifts their focus from a student not doing their homework to a student who seems to be struggling, they can move mountains.

With this particular student, I had gotten between him and another student and physically pushed them off one another. These students were not mine, I did not teach them, but I mentored them after school twice a week for over a year. I knew them and they confided in me. So when I saw his the-world-is-against-me attitude, I spoke to him as if he were my own son. I didn't write him up and wash my hands of him. I spoke to him because I cared for him. Sometimes, writing up a student is the easy way out. Cool teachers never take the easy way out – contrary to the beliefs of many stubborn colleagues.

I walked these students out to wait for their bus after school and the student I had spoken to had dropped back. I kept an eye on him as the students ran around and threw a football as they waited for their bus to arrive. It was only then that I realized that he was in line to board the same bus as the student with whom he tried to fight. I quickly walked over toward the line and called out his name. I motioned for him to come over to me, and, while keeping my gaze toward the line, I put my arm around his shoulder and spoke to him quietly enough for no one to hear, not to draw attention.

"Jayden, I don't know if you realize it, but I care about you doing well. When you get on that bus, I want you to keep your hands to yourself. Do you understand me?"

We stood next to each other, both looking straight ahead when he nodded yes.

"And Jayden, I don't know the last time someone told you this, but I am very proud of you." I glanced over at him, and I saw his eyes well up. I gave him a quick squeeze on the shoulder, then released him and walked away, never looking back. As I walked back into the building, I had to take a deep breath to fight back the tears as I said goodbye to the school secretary. I walked up the stairs to my classroom in silence. The halls were empty and dark. I walked into my room and sat at my desk for a spell. Then I got to work preparing my materials for an observation I was going to make the next morning.

The Takeaway

This is the extra mile. Giving your time to your students outside of your four walls. Treating your students as if they were your own kids, and the way that you hope a teacher would treat your kid should they ever make bad decisions. Whether it is giving up your prep period to scrub walls or, without the students realizing it, giving them that hug that they needed, students like the teachers whom they feel liked by. In my opinion, no adult should ever make a child feel disliked. Maybe *that* is what's not cool.

19

Don't Sink Like a Stone

No matter how young you are when you begin teaching, there will always be a time when the generation that you teach seems completely unlike your own. I see this struggle play out for many of my colleagues on a daily basis. It's easy to scoff at or even resent the generations that you cannot relate to. The longer you teach, the less you can relate. I have reflected on my own tendencies when I catch myself judging my students. It happens to us all. We were just like them and now we cannot imagine ever having been that student. Of course, we don't remember the times that the teachers who taught us had questioned our trends or listened in disappointment while we spoke freely about our priorities.

This blind spot, in my opinion, is due to the fact that we were kids. No matter how mature or self-disciplined we were as teenagers, there was always a time in that stage of life when the world seemed to revolve around you. Even the most aware and self-reflective students are operating with the brain of a teenager. I believe it to be pretty common knowledge that our frontal cortex does not finish developing until about the age of 25. This is the part of the brain that can consider long-term consequences. When a middle school or high school student makes a poor choice, it is partly due to the fact that they cannot conceive of the long-term effect. A 15-year-old thinks it's cool to get a tattoo, but they cannot grasp the concept that it is permanent. They know it is, but

DOI: 10.4324/9781003370161-22

"knowing" is very different from "understanding." Teenagers "know" everything.

I would often watch students, especially boys, unable to control themselves. Jumping up to hit the signs on the hallways, throwing a piece of eraser at a friend in class, or mixing the most disgusting concoction of liquids in lunch and daring one another to drink it. I would tell these students over and over again to make a different choice. They would express genuine regret and sometimes disappointment in their actions. Without fail, they would likely repeat the exact same behavior the next opportunity.

I had a student in class once, his name was Leo. Leo and his friend, Stephen, were always roughhousing, even during class. Leo struggled to stay in his seat no matter where I had him sit. He was drawn to his friend like my seven-year-old son was drawn to our cookie jar. Each class I would remind him to stay in his seat. Each class he would end up by Stephen at least twice. I finally began keeping tally marks of what I referred to kindly as "Leo attacks." I didn't do this to be mean, but it was simply mindblowing that this 13-year-old boy had not a clue that he was out of his seat routinely during class.

I pulled him into "my office" on multiple occasions to speak to him about his traveling show. He might control his impulses for the next 20 minutes, but then he would be up again. I had listened to a podcast and an audio book by a wonderful woman who was an expert in the "boy brain." She herself had raised three sons as a single mother and she seemed to have the insider perspective of what their minds were processing.

As the mother of a son, I found this author and doctor to be simply brilliant! Knowing about the development of a male brain and the tendency of boys to need movement, especially when processing new information, I began to sit back and observe the male students in my class. It was true, they did sprawl out of their desks and had to be in motion in some way, shape, or form. Many of them wanted to learn and were interested in the lesson, but, after so many minutes, they began to tune out my voice and find interest in their pen or their chair.

It was explained that not every male was the same. This woman referred to them as lambs or roosters. She used brain development and a great understanding of science to break it down to the level of a lay person. I understood that I was, in fact, raising a rooster in my own home. Additionally, I began to spot the roosters in my classrooms as well. I felt more sympathy for these boys when I realized that I wasn't witnessing a defiant student; rather, I was watching a teenage boy struggling to keep his need to move and his stimulated sensory in check. It became clear that they were at the mercy of their own biology. My mindset shifted.

Now I was wondering not how to discipline them, but how to accommodate that biological and developmental need so that they would be successful. I didn't tell Leo to stay in his seat, but I made him my paper passer and pencil sharpener. I let him walk to the tissue box, the garbage, and back while I was teaching without being offended. The Leo attacks became less, but they never stopped.

At one point I had heard in a podcast that males show affection through play. The speaker was referring to the animal world, and anyone who had a boy at home can relate. The roughhousing, tickle games, or tag games are a love language. Females seem to master their verbal expressions for affection, but boys say *we are friends* through flag football or play-fighting. I watched it with my own son and his father. No matter how fun I was as a mom, my son made the distinction between mom as affectionate and dad as play. His dad could wrestle with him or have a rambunctious tickle war with him, tossing him around the bed in ways I never could. My son not only wanted these moments, but he also needed them. It was clear to me that this was his bonding time with his dad or with any man in my family.

Next, my attention turned to my two male cats, Mozart and Waffles. Waffles would never leave Mozart alone. Waffles was a young four months old compared to Mozart's four years. At first, I assumed that Waffles was annoying Mozart. I even tried to intervene at times for the sake of Mozart. Eventually, it became clear to me that Mozart was enjoying these games. I even watched Mozart instigate it himself. These two cats were not fighting, they were playing. Additionally, both of them were seeking this interaction from the other. It was their love language and was as necessary and natural as a little girl hugging her stuffed animal.

By the end of the year, I came to see Stephen and Leo as my class cats. They were harmless, and they needed interaction with one another. I told them this, and they seemed to draw the same parallels as I had. By the time they came back to visit as eighth graders, they had moved beyond this stage of constant play and had become more aware of their female audience. I remember emailing their parents and letting them know that I appreciated their maturity to stop and focus when they needed to, but that they were just being boys who had an abundance of energy in class. I asked them if they could pass along the message that they must continue to keep the balance of fun and focus so that we all could have a successful year. The message was well received, and I think they appreciated their kids not being reprimanded constantly for their energy levels. Though I am not their teacher anymore, I often have two stray cats wander into my room after school just to say hello.

Another time I decided to adapt instead of pushing against student behavior was around 2015 when it seemed that every student in my class was into tapping their writing utensil on their desks in joint rhythm to create a class-wide jam session. At first, I found this behavior to be very annoying and very disruptive. If I asked them to stop, they would. However, this behavior of endlessly tapping their pens became a habit that most of them did not even seem to realize they were doing. If they were thinking while working, a steady plastic beat would begin to rise up. Some students were not tappers, they were clickers. These are the kids who clicked their pens endlessly. I often wondered if it was a mindless stress relief. I have noticed that the pen clicking, not the tapping, seemed to be more common in the districts where my kids had more challenges at home.

Instead of continually yelling, or handing out lunch detention slips like birthday party invitations, I knew I had to come up with another way to address the behavior. It was insidious. It became an unconscious habit that proliferated in every class, and I watched colleagues struggle with it as well. I began to consider my options so that I was not swimming upstream the entire year. This district had many more serious behavior issues, and tapping a pen was not going to be the action toward which I put my energy. It became clear that some of these students were indeed very talented and their beats were quite impressive. Sure, it was a pen and a desk, so it seemed unimpressive at first, but if they were wielding a drumstick on a drum, these cats would be impressive!

I made a deal with my pen tappers. I gave them the last five minutes of class to create a "tap circle" if they refrained from doing it in class. Not only did this work, but also their display of skills at the end of class was quite awesome. Other students began trying to learn or join in. It was very similar to a rhythmic drum circle. Enthusiasm ran high, and so I opened my lunch (which I already had about 20 kids in my room for) to these tappers, so to speak. I must admit that these are definitely some of my fondest memories. It was, dare I say, almost beautiful to watch all these students of mine across my classes get together and create a sound that seemed to breathe from the collaborative creativity. For those minutes, I saw the potential of teamwork. I watched them take turns leading the circle and allowing space for others to shine.

As far as the clickers went, they were not so easy to solve. I found myself clicking my pen as I was teaching more than once and so I understood the mindless nature of it. I was teaching about Mesopotamia one day and a student was incessantly clicking away on his pen. Without breaking from my lesson and in a very casual fashion I walked over to the tape sitting on my desk, still teaching, and over to the student's desk. Again, without pausing my lesson, I continued to teach from the side of his desk as I took his pen and taped down the top so the pen was able to write but could no longer be clicked. I handed it back and walked back up to the board. I did so mindlessly and did not consider how odd it must have been. My students began laughing and I looked at the owner of the pen as he stared at his newfangled utensil in awe.

This became "The Matusz Treatment," and, despite some students trying to get the treatment just for attention, it worked rather well. In fact, later in my career, if a student was not disrupting the lesson but was simply clicking away, I would pull the same move – same smoothness, same matter-of-factness – just to watch the reaction of the class. It was during these short moments when I would inject some sort of silliness or randomness into my classes that were most memorable to my students.

The Takeaway

♦ Repurpose their disruptive behavior. Some teachers set aside the last two minutes of class for a student to tell jokes or teach dance moves. There is a well-known American comedian named Jim Carrey who is famous for his goofy, energetic, oddball skits. He has told the story that when he was in seventh grade, if he was good all day, his teacher gave him the last 15 minutes of class to perform. He said he would make jokes about life and school and do faculty impressions. Can you imagine? These are the decisions that need to be measured in secondary education; some students have a personality or a habit that is not conducive to an orderly learning environment. In college they may teach you to use discipline or force the student into the mold in which you need them to be. If you have not learned yet, this strategy is horrible for both you and the student. Strike that deal or find that balance that accepts the reality of the situation but does the least amount of damage to your teaching. Otherwise, you will be in a battle royal for the entire year. If not for the student, figure something out for your own sake. Make the expectations and boundaries clear and hold firm to them. If Jim Carrey was not "good all day" by his teacher's expectations, then I am guessing he didn't get to do what he was most passionate about.

♦ Not every student will become an academic or go on to pursue a college career. Imagine what the world would have lost if our great comedians were stifled and forced into conformity. Maybe a teacher's definition of success is good grades, but maybe our definition is exclusive to some walks of life. Our artists, musicians, inventors, comedians, and many others are defined by academic success, and thank goodness for that! Without the varieties of neurodivergence and talent, our world may be full of over-achievers in academics and yet lack all of the beautiful types of minds that inspire us so often. If a student is disruptive, do what you need to do, but whatever that looks like for your classroom, please, do not be the adult that extinguishes their fire. Your classwork should never trump a student's passion and success, even if it's not defined by getting an A in your class.

20

"Get Real" Talk

Many teachers are a decade or more older than their students. This makes us wise, good sources of advice, and able to appreciate the mistakes of our younger students. However, this also makes us "old" and "out of touch" with our kiddos. If a teacher has a child at home who is also a teenager, then we have the best cheat code ever! However, not all teachers have this child. Maybe your child isn't as old as the students you teach, is older, or you don't have a child! I have some thoughts on how you can keep your finger on the pulse of the society your students are living in.

If nothing else, I think that we all are aware that social media is a definite departure from when we were teenagers. If you can focus on just this one factor alone, you will be able to empathize with your students and get a glimpse into their world.

First, once a year, usually about two months into the year so that students feel safe, I will have them answer the journal prompt: *What do you wish adults understood about how it is to be a teenager today?* Teenagers have a reputation for not wanting to talk about their "feelings," but I have found the opposite. Some students will not volunteer their response, but will most likely shake their head in agreement with those who do. I find that teens want to talk...all the time. They just don't want to talk to their parents or to the adults who, they feel, are not listening.

At this point you have already established that you are a caring and genuine teacher. Therefore, you may be amazed at what

DOI: 10.4324/9781003370161-23

they have to tell you. In my experience with this question I often get the following answers from my students over the last few years:

♦ We have too much on our plates – we have to be good at sports and get straight A's
♦ We feel a lot of anxiety around being good enough for our parents
♦ We get bullied all of the time on social media by people making mean comments on our posts
♦ It's hard to do well in school with all of these tests
♦ We are always accused of being on our devices too much
♦ Society thinks we are selfish or dumb
♦ I have too many responsibilities
♦ There's too much pressure to look and act a certain way

Some of these comments are pretty universal and can describe any teenage experience. However, I do believe from my discussions around this prompt that social media is causing so much anxiety and feelings of not being "good enough." I have had the experience of teaching when cell phones in the school were welcomed, and the policy was "bring your own device." We encouraged cell phones so students could use them for Internet access. Obviously, this was a time before students were each given a device; rather, we had a cart of chromebooks that was shared among seven teachers. They were as sought-after as the hot new celebrity, but they never performed to the purpose – they were always uncharged or unable to connect to the Wi-Fi.

So I witnessed first-hand the change in students from "cell phones are great!" to "put that evil device away!" Students became more reserved, making friends via social media rather than in person. There was even a term for this, a VBFF (Virtual Best Friend Forever). These friends were extremely close in texts and in social media messages but not in person at school. I saw this strange parallel reality begin to form in my classroom. Eye contact became less frequent, volunteers disappeared, "good mornings" went away and so did bold personalities. It seemed like someone replaced my students with overly tired and socially awkward versions of themselves.

Lunchrooms became quieter as students were all looking down at their devices, often texting their real-life friend who was within speaking distance. They looked more paranoid or self-aware, as all the BUZZING and DINGING went off around them. *Are they talking about me? Who is it that is texting my friend about me?*

As a member of the millennial generation (1984), I also was addicted to checking my phone. Messages were always distracting, then it became Facebook, and even Twitter for my news alerts. Yet, my confidence hadn't really changed. I may have had the same tech tendencies as my students, yet they seemed more like ghosts. After many of these journal prompt discussions, I realized what the difference was between my generation and theirs. Why I was still able to walk into a room confidently after being on social media, but they were not. This is what I began to do after this journal prompt. This may not fit into all subject areas, but it could be used as a social and emotional skill-building lesson. Such lessons are welcomed in most classrooms.

1. I stand (bravely) in front of the class and tell the students to take a minute of silence and look at me as if I am a photo of one of their peers on social media. I tell them to think of the types of not nice comments that I would read about myself. I encourage them to be as honest as possible because I want to know what it is that they hear all of the time that adults do not understand.
2. After that very long and slightly uncomfortable silent minute, I ask students to raise their hands and let me hear what "other peers" their age may post about my appearance – clothes, hair, makeup, body shaming, shoes, *let it all out* I tell them.
3. Next, and this is the hardest part, without any feedback (unless it's school inappropriate), I write every comment on the board. If they seem "too nice" I egg them on, "Come on. This is really the type of stuff you guys hear?" Then they really start to lean into it.

Too skinny
Not skinny enough
You probably have an eating disorder
You wear too much makeup
Your makeup is all wrong
Your shaved undercut means that you are gay
You are poor and that's why you have a paper mask (yes, even my COVID mask was targeted)
You wear the same shoes everyday
Your shoes look like paper bags for lunch
Your tattoos mean that your parents don't love you
You're a dumb blonde
Your figure isn't what is popular (an appropriate way of saying that I'm built like a pole)
 There's no way that you could be an athlete
 You are a teacher's pet
 Your hair doesn't match your outfit
 Your clothes are old and outdated (more on this in another chapter!)
 You can't fight
 You have no eyebrows (true)
 You need braces
 Your nails are ugly
You probably listen to Country music (ironically, I do not, but is that an insult?)
Your tattoos mean you do drugs
Your nose is too big (possibly)
You're a Russian spy (a rumor that continued for a few months)
Your lips aren't big enough
Your laugh is horrible (even though this was a "picture" of me …)
You're a Karen (aka white racist woman)
You're probably racist (again, an observation made based on only my appearance)

The list went on. One year a student told me that I looked like a junkie version of Cinderella and that my dress was like a gay pride parade. It is a social experiment that often says more about the observer than you. Though I still suggest that you are in a strong mental space on the day that you give this exercise!

All of these critiques are written on the board in front of the room. Now, I begin to explain to the students why my generation isn't as traumatized as theirs from social media. Not because we use it less, not because we are less consumed by drama, but because we grew up in silence. I got my first cellphone when I was 17, not because my parents had a policy against it but because they simply weren't around and affordable until then!

So what? Well, that means that me and others my age (38) grew up during the most formative and vulnerable years of middle and high school without this chatter. Unless someone said something to you directly, or a rumor spread, you were often blissfully oblivious to these insults and judgments. I am not suggesting that bullying wasn't bad in my generation, it happened just like it does today with a few major differences.

1. Usually there was the one or few actual bullies who would say the horrible things, and the spineless followers would just laugh or stay silent. Not often did the entire school sprout these insults. Those who stood by and did nothing were awful, but they were but silent.
2. The bullying happened when you were out of your house most likely.

    Today, our students who are being subjected to these nasty words are reading them in their living room, in their bathroom, at their dinner table, before they go to sleep, and when they wake up in the morning. This generation has no reprieve. Bullied students can be so badly tormented that they skip school. Movies from the 1980s and 1990s like *The Neverending Story* come to mind. The target of the school's hate hides away, never truly going to school as they told their parents they were. They avoided the place of abuse.

    Our students have no place to hide. It is constant and even more vicious.
3. A person always grows bolder and meaner the farther away they are from their target.

Think about road rage and Internet trolls. These people will say some of the most abhorrent things to another human being, mostly because they are actually protected by the distance between them and their victim of choice. Ever drive with someone who curses out and gives the finger to any drive that really pisses them off? However, the same person avoids actual conflict or is not nearly as aggressive in their day-to-day interactions? I call it "Road Muscles," akin to "Beer Muscles." These tyrants get more emboldened because they have a false sense of rage and righteousness when there is distance between them. Do you ever see the object of their road rage pull over or get out of their car? Amazing how quickly the bully puts up the window or suddenly has to get to their destination immediately.

This trolling phenomenon is what is happening to our students. Some of the things that they read or "hear" on a daily basis are intolerable for most people, never mind a teenager whose only priority in life is to blend in with their peers and get their approval. Teenagers have long been known to risk their safety in order to impress their peers. Imagine if I stood in front of my class and they told me the same exact things but instead of being their teacher of 38 years of age, I am a kid during this approval-seeking time in my life when the value of my peers' opinions means more to me than the love and accolades of my parents – assuming I had two loving, involved parents.

It was cringeworthy as an adult who knew my value and formed my sense of self during a time that hurtful things did not follow me around in my pocket all day, every day, even on vacation or in the safety of my own home.

This is what I do:

I tell my students to close their eyes and put their heads down on their desks. "All I want you to do is listen, no noises or remarks. Let my voice fill the silence in the room, and listen to it." I then read each comment I wrote back to them. I don't say them in a nasty voice, I stay calm, and just read them off as if it was a grocery list, giving each one a second to fill the silence, to be heard.

Next, I wait a few seconds and ask them to raise their heads. I ask them: Is this what you hear all around you all day, every day? Some students have tears in their eyes, and quickly my amusing bashing hits very close to home for them. They nod in agreement, and I then tell them what I had already revealed. These words are in your school bus, your parents' car, your dining room, and maybe even your shower or bedroom.

I then explain, "See, the difference between you and I is that I was able to get a reprieve from all the haters around me. I didn't hear a stream of criticisms during all of my waking hours. In fact, I often was completely unaware of what anyone thought of me, unless they had told me. Do you go up to students and say all the things you comment on? Are all the comments you read spoken to you face to face by each author?

There is power in looking at someone's eyes when you speak to them. When you can see the pain in a person's face, you can witness the pain you are causing them immediately in real time. You realize the truth in your words, the damage they can cause when directed at a person. Yet, on social media we don't have to see our peers cry in their bedrooms when your comment pops up under their post. You don't hear their parents talking about how concerned they are about the dramatic change in their child's once happy demeanor, do you? No. You get a rush from the hateful things you write, maybe you even feel more perfect when you type them. The next day at school, you never even pass this person or at the very least speak to them. Yet, you do not hesitate to send them off to sleep with brutal comments each night.

The difference is: I was able to grow up through my formative years and forge my sense of self without hearing all of these things that you just heard. That is why my generation can take social risks and be funny or ungraceful. I can be silly as your teacher and make jokes or be very passionate about something without wondering if you think I'm "cool." Because I know who I am and I discovered who I was without anyone else's opinions invading my thoughts all day long, making me question myself and my self-worth. Maybe I have no right to be as confident and sure of myself as I am. But this is the beauty of growing up in a largely silent world. No one can take away my confidence today because it was forged through my own judgments, my family's love, and the dear friends who would never have hurt me the way some people can hate perfect strangers today.

I wish that I could give you what I had. I cannot, but I can tell you that the sooner you get off social media, the sooner you stop looking for everyone's likes, follows, or approval, the closer you will become to the person you truly are in life. And this, my friends, will become your truth and soon you may find that all the worry and anxiety that you carried around have fallen off of your shoulders. Because now you walk into a room confident of who you are – not what others think you are. This power of perspective will change your life, and you can all do it.

The Takeaway

♦ SEL, or Social Emotional Learning, has become more of a focus in schools. These are the types of lessons that teach empathy, responsible use of social media, anti-bullying, and many more things. Often teachers are asked to teach SEL-focused lessons during a non-academic class. Discussions like these may be useful for those instances or on half-days before holiday breaks. I have a study hall, the other half of lunch when students sit in my room and are able to do work. Contractually, we are not allowed to be tasked with instruction during this class. If you ever think that this lesson might be beneficial, then may be a good time to teach it. It does not need to be formal, but it can make an impact.

♦ There is a power in acknowledging the challenging environment these students must navigate each day. Allowing them the space to feel heard or to share the impact social media has had on them can be extremely beneficial. Never has this discussion ever become inappropriate, and, as the adult in the room, you can set the tone of discussion expectations. If this seems risky for you, then do not use it. I have found that by the time I may decide to have this discussion, I have built a strong foundation with my students based on respect. The importance of respect and the clarity of your purpose leading this discussion are most important. Each year there is unfortunately an incident that occurs surrounding cyber-bullying. This is when I consider doing this activity, but I always make sure that it is clear. Never should a student feel uncomfortable in your class, and you know your students best. Read the room. When done successfully, it establishes both you and your classroom as a safe place, and that is the ultimate purpose.

21

The Power of Choice

The power of choice is something that is often alluded to in the field of education. You can find it in cookie-cutter choice boards, which were once hailed as the be all and end all of cutting-edge curriculum. I always found the pre-made choice boards to be very simplistic, and, in an era when the depth of knowledge or the Costa Levels of Questioning is so emphasized, these novel ideas do not seem to have much depth to them. Oftentimes they offer topical actions that can be applied to any content at any level. Though I loved the concept of choice, I approached it from the "grade what you tell" concept.

I taught seventh grade ELA for five years, and, though I love teaching ELA, the novels that you teach in class are the crux of the curriculum. If you are in a school or a grade whose reading materials have novels that are not great, or relatable to the students, then it's a bad curriculum. When I finally got a position as an eighth grade Social Studies teacher, even notes were exciting to teach. I was excited about the content and passionate about storytelling. It was not as easy to be passionate about commas in a series or conjunctive adverbs – unless, they were in the context of a great novel like *The Outsiders* or the stories of Edgar Allan Poe. The book selection really makes or breaks the passion.

As a lover of all things historical, I could make all of my textbook content fascinating because I found it fascinating. However, there are so many concepts to teach when covering an entire

DOI: 10.4324/9781003370161-24

civilization. From government to culture to religion to any number of military actions, the content is vast and can present a challenge when assessing the unit. Often a unit test in Social Studies became a memorization task filled with names, dates, and events. I preferred not to test my students this way. I wanted more from them. I wanted them to specialize in one aspect of civilization and also to be able to make connections from ancient lives to modern lives.

I had to build my assessment backward from the objective to the task. If I wanted them to demonstrate their understanding of the civilization, they had many options from which to choose to do so. Not every student is an avid essay writer nor good at memorizing facts for an objective exam. My solution was to combine multiple ways for them to demonstrate their comprehension to me. First, there would be a written piece. Depending on their choice, this could be a summary, essay, or description. Next, there had to be a basic understanding of the major people and events. So there would be an objective multiple-choice component that gave them the ability to choose eight out of twelve questions to answer.

Then they were given a "choice board" with options for them to demonstrate their understanding of the unit. This is where that written "description" piece is used. Say if they chose to make pottery from ancient Mesopotamia, they also had to include an index card describing the item (think museum plaque), the materials used, the design, the purpose it was used for, and how the design reflects the time period. Other options were a map of the city-state identifying the types and locations of buildings and any other important details of the city planning. A "newspaper" from the time reporting an event that we had read about with whimsical advertisements, a model ziggurat accompanied by an explanation of purpose and design, a diary from a Mesopotamian describing life. Since Mesopotamians wrote in cuneiform, I made the students write in cuneiform in the diary and in at least one section of the newspaper. To this day, I still have cards written to me by former students in cuneiform.

Choice is important not only in assessing your students; the power of choice can also make all the difference when a student feels cornered. If a student is making a bad choice, we already know that their brain is not able to really make decisions for long-term success yet. However, they always have the power of choice. When I called students into my office, I first asked how they were doing. If they were still in a state of anger or not open to listening to me, I would always provide them with a choice.

"You have choices here. One choice is to continue doing what you've been doing in class. and I will have to take the next action for discipline, or you can go get a drink from the fountain and walk back into the room without disrupting anyone. If you need to put your head down, that's fine, but what you cannot choose to do is disrupt the lesson because other kids are really interested in learning today. You can think about it, but I need you back in the room within a minute."

The teenage brain is conditioned to push back against authority and challenge the status quo. I am not a neuroscientist, but I do remember some of my Adolescent Development course that I had to take in order to be highly qualified to teach secondary school in New Jersey. At first, I figured it was another scheme of the Education Department to take money from their teachers, but it absolutely benefited me. If your state doesn't mandate this for secondary educators, I would recommend reading or listening to podcasts on your own time. The teenage brain is not what we operate with (assuming you are older than 26), and though we all like to tell our students that we were also teenagers at one point, all one needs to do is read a diary or letter from your secondary years to understand just how dramatic and short-sighted we were. Heck, I got married at 23 and thought I knew what forever meant. Just like that marriage, even the most obviously bad decisions aren't so obvious to the young brain.

If you do not believe in the power that giving a choice has, see what happens when you tell your students that they can sit wherever they want in class. Even the most chill high school student will light up for a moment. Why? Well, think about it …

Depending on the school where you teach, students are expected to follow rules all day long with very little autonomy. Even in the laxest of schools, think about the expectations that students are held to and which they are unable to disobey without consequences:

- ◆ Walk in the halls
- ◆ Walk quietly in the halls
- ◆ Walk THIS way (some are one-directional) in the halls
- ◆ Sit still
- ◆ Look up at the teacher
- ◆ Ask permission to use the bathroom
- ◆ Only use the bathroom at these times and this many times
- ◆ Raise your hand to speak
- ◆ Raise your hand to sharpen a pencil
- ◆ Copy my notes right now the way I write them
- ◆ Read right now
- ◆ Answer the question I ask you
- ◆ Do not tap your pencil
- ◆ Do not swing your feet
- ◆ Put your feet on the floor
- ◆ Pick your head up
- ◆ Do not make eye contact with your friend
- ◆ Do not turn around to talk to a friend
- ◆ Do not talk at all unless given permission
- ◆ Do not wear the clothes that violate our code
- ◆ Do not wear a hat
- ◆ Do not wear makeup that may distract others
- ◆ Boys, pull up your pants
- ◆ Girls, your cleavage is distracting the boys
- ◆ Take your hood down
- ◆ Be quicker because you will be late
- ◆ Eat your lunch in 20 minutes
- ◆ Be kind to every other teenager in the school
- ◆ Be respectful to all adults
- ◆ Clean up your lunch trash
- ◆ Calm down and don't be so loud
- ◆ Wait until the bell rings to pack up your belongings
- ◆ Sit still until I dismiss you
- ◆ Do not chew gum
- ◆ Do not look at your phone or watch

- ◆ Do not snack outside of lunch
- ◆ Do not have coffee
- ◆ Do not have anything to drink other than water
- ◆ Do not hand out candy or gum to friends

And for goodness sake, stop rolling your eyes and look like you're happy to be here!!

These are just the average number of rules we impose on students in many secondary schools. I have taught in a charter school where uniforms were imposed down to the belt and shoe color and design. Students were expected to be completely silent when moving in the halls in the formation of a single-file line. This school was built on expectations and rules, so the students had to follow my orders as if they were in the military. One word made them pack up their books, another had them stand at their desks, and the third dismissed them from a particular side of their desks. They even had to pass papers a specific way. To me, I felt like I was institutionalizing the kids, as if they were in a military academy or, worse, a jail. Everything was controlled, and in order for them to be successful in this system they had to conform and follow all commands.

Now, a normal teenager is wired to rebel and find their own identity in the world. Conforming is the exact opposite of what they are biologically driven to do during this period of their lives. Elementary students might respond very well to such directives and structure. I do not understand the complete failure of our educational system to recognize this flaw of contrarian demands. I once read that for a teenager, waking up at 6 am for school was the equivalent of adults waking up at 3 am. They are literally growing their brains, and so, just like a developing infant, they need to sleep. Isn't it bad enough that we are already fighting their natural circadian rhythm? Tired, groggy, and, if they are males, often starving for constant calories, we expect them to enter the school in a completely amicable frame of mind and willing to follow every rule we have imposed. It's a miracle that teenagers don't go around yelling at teachers all day. If that seems like a wild statement, clearly you have not witnessed your wonderful child morph into a teenage creature before your very own eyes.

Due to the nature of our careers, teachers are often sitting in professional development sessions or faculty meetings. Think back to your last meeting with your colleagues. How many of them checked their cell phones? How many of them were on their laptop working? How many of them were talking when they weren't supposed to or not sitting with their feet on the floor and backs straight in their chairs? Did anyone walk out to use the restroom? And how many rolled their eyes or snickered at some comment or piece of news? These are our peers, adults. Adults with a completely formed brain with all the lived experience and lessons of the adolescent years behind us – adults who should be able to refrain from these behaviors for the length of a meeting. A meeting that may be only an hour or four, not the average six hours that our students sit through. Imagine one of your more vocal colleagues who likes to challenge the status quo being required to play basketball in the gym. Though it may be fun to visualize for a moment, the reality is that they would most likely refuse to if they did not *want* to.

The Takeaway

♦ I have found that I have a difficult time sitting still and giving my undivided attention at my meetings. I am guilty of all of the above behaviors. Yet, we expect this restrained behavior from the very brains that are meant to move, socialize, and challenge the status quo. I am not suggesting that you throw out all of the rules, but I am suggesting that you choose which of your classroom rules are most important to you. Does it matter if a student has their foot on a chair in class while taking notes? Is chewing gum really an infraction, or does it help the ADHD student concentrate as they do their work? If a student puts up their hood in my room, will it prevent my other students from learning? These are the real questions that teachers need to answer before they begin the school year. Some say pick your battles; I say let go of the control and be aware of your audience. If you don't know them, then how are you teaching them in the most effective way? Teach *yourself* about your students if you are not aware of these crucial developmental years.

◆   On a side note, when I give a student a choice to return to my room and not distract the class or I will have to take the next disciplinary step, I am purposefully being vague about that next step. My brother is an administrator, and he once taught me this gem. Never commit to a disciplinary action that you hold over a student because if it should change or if you should change your mind, you will never have credibility again. Should a teacher threaten detention or a phone call home and not follow through 100% of the time, they've lost their leverage. A teenager can smell blood in the water – your weakness not to follow through with your threat. In order to never follow through with your word, keep it vague.

22

The Toughest Ones
Need You the Most

To me, it was this simple. The students who seemed to work really hard to get thrown out of my classes were the ones I refused to send to the office for their behavior (assuming at all times that this behavior isn't a threat or egregious).

I once was working for a company that required me to travel and listen to keynote speakers in the field of education. I was in San Diego, CA, when I heard this administrator talk about how difficult he was as a student. He said that he was angry, poor, and overwhelmed. He had a teacher who seemed to care about him more than any other teacher he had ever had before. One particularly bad day, he flipped his desk at this teacher and walked out of her room, taking all of his anger out on her.

Why? Why would someone take out their anger on the person who, they felt, cared about them so much? Think about it. Why is it OK if your own child tells you that they "hate you," out of anger? You wouldn't accept that from a total stranger or maybe even a student. Have you ever gotten home from a long day of work and when your partner interacts with you, you become short with them? Maybe they tell you that you seem irritated or ask what's wrong and you just shrug it off and give no explanation.

DOI: 10.4324/9781003370161-25

That man did what he did to that special teacher who cared for him because he knew he could. He felt safe. In his story, this man went on to say that it was the end of the year and he was so upset that he would never see this particular teacher again that he acted out these feelings with aggression and anger. He had not had the maturity or the language to express how upset it made him, so he acted with the only emotion he knew, aggression.

As he had trusted, this teacher didn't write him up or have him expelled. Instead, she started the next day and the last day of school as if nothing had happened. I am sure as a teacher that she had checked on him or called security when this occurred, but as far as he had known, she didn't try to "get him in trouble" for it.

I wish I had remembered this man's name because his story was full of emotion and I was overwhelmed by his honesty. In him, I saw many of my students at the time. Tough, angry, feeling as if it's them against the world. Every so often I would be on the receiving end of their rage. It hurt my feelings more than it made me angry. I too, like this man's teacher, would follow up or check in on them, but I wouldn't take any punitive action against them. I knew that they had more on their shoulders at the young age of 15 than I had, and I wanted to know what it was that made them give up at that moment. I wanted to help them get back on track.

This mystery keynote speaker struck a chord with me. He closed his speech by stating that he was at a point in his life when he thought he wasn't worth anything – that he was a failure, a burden, and that no one wanted him.

The act of throwing the desk at this trusted teacher was in his words a way to "prove himself right," to show himself that not even this teacher who cared about him would want to deal with his antics.

He was proven wrong. Though he thought that he had wanted to prove himself right, when he found out that she hadn't written him up and instead seemed to forgive him without judgment – well, that's when this grown man began to cry on stage. That is what I have never forgotten.

The students that goof-off the most or tap their fingers and pencils endlessly, those who ask to get up or walk around to sharpen their pencils, these are the ones who seem to be shout-ing, "Hey! Here I am, please see me." And so, when a student flipped a desk in class (which happened more than a few times in my career), I asked them to step into my office. In a calm, con-trolled manner I would ask them if they were OK. More than once, this "violent" student would begin to cry.

The Takeaway

♦   There is no practical use for this lesson. No matter what you may have to say to convince both the student and yourself that you want them to go back into the room and try to start over, you say it. You say it because you do care, and you don't want this child to fail. You say it because the ones who are the toughest are the ones who need you the most, and they need you to tell them that you are not giving up on them.

♦   I had a particularly distracting student in my eighth grade history class. He was 15 and had already been left behind in elementary school, and it seemed like he was far away from passing again. He avoided all work. Other teachers of his would complain about his inability to focus or that he didn't take class seriously and was more concerned with his social life.

In an attempt to find out why he wrote so tiny (a sign I've noticed of small confidence. If a student writes so small or so sloppy that you can't read it, then you cannot see all their misspelled words), I went to his teacher who taught Read 180. I knew he was on a low reading level, but I wanted to see how he was writing in her class and with her help.

It turned out that, yes, though she was the Read 180 teacher and taught him reading, this student was on such a low level that he was below the Read 180 materials. She had to ask for books that were used in an old elemen-tary program in the district to teach him reading.

When she showed me his work, he was matching letters to sounds. I don't know about you, but, at 15, most of us would rather look "cool" than "dumb." This student acted like he could care less because he was illiterate. It was his secret that he had kept away from his friends and guarded at all costs against any teacher who seemed to threaten to put him in a position to expose it. This is the simple reason why I never make students read in class or show their work without their consent.

23

Step into My Office

When I began teaching in Cumberland County, NJ, prior to that I had only taught in central New Jersey (though this location seems to be disputed) in the town of Jackson. My first year was abysmal. I was the fourth teacher in the room by October, and I had no experience teaching in a poverty-stricken area. I knew I wanted to go into urban education, but I had graduated from college during the "Great Recession" and so I had been out of my college classes for over six years at that point!

I was given a real run for my money as my students made it known that, before I arrived, there had been no consistency, and they began to run the room themselves. I, like many new teachers, would spend some afternoons after the kids left sitting at my desk completely shell-shocked and, at times, even in tears.

I could not hit my "swag" and the kids seemed to hate me. I had three 80-minute classes, two of them were good, but the last one was awful. I can quite clearly remember the moment I realized the mistake that I was making that allowed the students to seemingly gain an upper hand over me. I dreaded this last class of the day –each week it was a power struggle of 1 versus 28. It was exhausting, thank goodness I was a mere 25 years old and had the "I can save the world" mindset!

So here is the rookie mistake that I made and have since never made again. It went something like this:

DOI: 10.4324/9781003370161-26

Student A: "This work sucks, I'm not doing it."
Me: "What did you say, Student A?"
Student A: "I didn't say anything."
Me: "Please stop interrupting my lesson."
Student B: "He didn't say anything."
Me: "OK …"
Student C: "I don't like this lesson."
Students A and B: LAUGHING
Me: "Friends, please be quiet."
Student B: MAKES A NOISE
Me: "Student B, stop making noises."
Student A: "He didn't make a noise."
Student C: MAKES A NOISE
Me: If any of you want to make noises, then you can go to the vice principal's office."
Student A: "oooooooooooooo"
Whole Class: "ooooooooooooooo"
Students B and C: "Ok, come on, let's go, I don't care."
Students A, B, and C walk out of my room on their own discretion.
Me: "OK, class let's get back to what we were learning."
Rest of Class: WHISPERING AND LAUGHING

This should never have happened. First, no student should feel that they have the authority to walk out of my room, especially three of them! Second, no student should *want* to walk out of my room!

This is where I failed; however, from it I drew the best lesson I ever learned. All secondary students in general (meaning teenagers) are cognitively designed at that stage of development to cherish the opinion of their peers over anything else – over family, over authority, over safety, over personal gain. Let that sink in. Adolescents look for the approval of their peers. So if students A, B, and C wouldn't necessarily choose their own family over impressing their friends, then why in the world would they be concerned about a teacher's ultimatum?

Now, this is not to suggest that teenagers are shallow, selfish, evil spawns. Quite the opposite, this is also a time in their development when they begin to care about the world around them and challenge things they view to be unjust.

The key concept to understand here is that they need the *approval* of their peers.

This is the loophole, and this is when I decided that I would have an "office" right outside my classroom door. In addition, I explained this procedure to my classes in the beginning days of the school year when it came time to discuss the respect factor and my expectations.

This is best done in real time through role-playing. I can explain the concept here: Students, plainly, need to "save face," that is, keep their reputation in the eyes of their peers. So the worst thing, that which adds the fuel to the flame, is when a teacher disciplines a student in front of their peers. This goes back to the "do you earn respect" factor. If I am in a store line and the cashier calls me out by reprimanding me in front of all the other customers, I walk out upset, maybe even furious. Maybe I even correct them for their rudeness.

Now, if the same cashier quietly gets my attention and gives me an immediate "out" or excuse by saying (in a calm and low tone), "Ma'am, I am open if you are ready," I am not embarrassed because she gave me a reason to have not been paying attention: I wasn't ready. Even though I am aware I was on my phone or was spacing out, this person offered me a way to maintain my pride in front of others.

Reviewing this (as I will demonstrate) in the respect talk on the first few days is crucial because then there is no need to explain during the moment when it is happening:

Student A: "This work sucks, I'm not doing it."
Me: OK, friends, I'd like to take a brain break, so I want you to turn to a partner and play RPS best out of five (by this time you should know what type of task you can give students so that you can step "out" of the room. I have had some amazing students that I could assign work to as I go into my "office").

I QUIETLY WALK TOWARD STUDENT A AND ASK HIM/ HER/THEY TO STEP INTO MY OFFICE FOR A MOMENT

1) I was discrete.
2) I keep an eye on the class with the door propped open but with Student A out of their view.
3) Students were given a task so they are distracted but monitored.
4) Furthermore, when students begin asking them what happens when you get back into the room, be the gatekeeper for that student and let the class know it's not for them to worry about. This helps them to not have to act out again and protects their privacy. It goes a long way when they feel like you are on their side.

Now, the student is in front of me, my body language is relaxed, and I ASK this question: "Are you OK? You seem a little off today, anything going on that you need to talk to someone about?"

The magic here lies in the act of **asking** if a student is OK. Our students are usually awesome kids, and one on one they won't challenge you because the audience of their peers is no longer a factor in their decisions. Furthermore, you may be alarmed to find out that you were the last teacher they had that day but the first and only one to ask if they were OK even though they may have been thrown out of their previous classes throughout the day.

Teenagers are not biologically mean; sometimes they don't know how to process things and so it comes out as defiance. Anyone with a teenage child can attest that they may have been the victim of their averted anger. Even more important, in districts that suffer from poverty, students are often experiencing some heady stuff that they carry each day. When I give my respect talk, I often remind them that even though I am older than they, many of them have experienced things that I have never had to experience at my age, and maybe never will.

The Takeaways

- ◆ Our students are resilient, but we must always keep their strength in mind when we may be quick to call them out for disrupting a lesson. Yes, we teachers are people with our own problems, but teaching is our career. To many of our students your lesson is just another hour of their day filled with many more interactions, responsibilities, grief, frustrations, etc. Remember the talk about getting off your pedestal? This is the right moment to put your lesson aside for a moment to check in on your student.

  Without exaggeration, nine out of ten times my student was completely disarmed by my question and was apologetic. Even if they didn't want to talk, I would ask them not to disrupt the lesson because it's really important. There are several scenarios here that can happen, but afterward, they always walked back into the class and sat down without an issue. From then on, it was a matter of eye contact if they began seeking attention from their peers in a negative way again.

- ◆ Some scenarios I have come across while in "my office" ended with me following up with:
  - I want you to stay in my room because I really enjoy the things you add to my lessons, can you please come back in and not disrupt the rest of the students?
  - I understand that you may not want to talk to me, but you definitely don't seem like your normal happy self today. I want you to walk to the water fountain, take a few breaths, and then come back in to reset yourself. I want to see that smile!
  - I have bad days too, believe me this morning was really hard for me. How about you can come back into the room, but instead of challenging me or disrupting the lesson you can put your head down for a few minutes to reset. I need you in my room, but I also need to teach this lesson to your peers. Can we agree on this?

If you feel comfortable talking to someone, I'm always here or I can reach out to the counselor.

- Listen, I get that schoolwork isn't always fun for you, and I'm kind of embarrassed to say, I put a lot of thought and planning into this lesson. You may not want to do it, but I was certainly excited to teach it and I think some of your peers are ready to do the work, too. Trust me when I tell you it has a purpose, and we will have a more "free form" lesson soon. Come on, let's get back in there.

24

I Am Your Teacher for Life

I am sure that this seems daunting to some of you and even terrifying for our students. Yet, it is something I always tell my kids and something that I have found to be true.

Remember when students defined a good teacher as the one who cares about them, not just in their class? That's the answer to building your student rapport. When was the last time that you asked a student of yours how they did on a test in another class? Have you checked in to see why they never turned in that science project that their teacher left in your mailbox for them to complete?

As teachers, if our kids are not successful, then we are not successful. Now, I don't mean that they get straight A's; I mean that they believe that they are capable. I taught history, but you bet if I was staying after school and I knew a student hadn't turned in an assignment for another class that they were in my room working on it. It takes a village to raise a child – it takes a lot more than that to keep a teenager on track.

Other examples of being a teacher for life may be when I found out that two of my students wanted to fight and that one of them would've been expelled permanently from the district had he fought again. This specific student wanted to be a police officer when he grew up, but he had a very tough life and a brother who was in a violent gang. He witnessed violence and was the victim

DOI: 10.4324/9781003370161-27

of abuse himself. No wonder he thought to solve all his problems by fighting. It was the model he was raised with.

I see my "kids" as my kids, and I wasn't going to let this bright young man throw his opportunities out the door with his fists. I sat with him and talked with him during my prep (yes, he was late to his next class), and he told me that he really didn't want to fight but he had to. Once again, it's all about keeping a reputation among their peers and, often, their families as well. So I spent the rest of my preps and my lunch moderating between my two students. I escorted them to and from classes so that a fight couldn't be instigated. By the end of the day, they had signed a peer mediation contract that would keep them from speaking about fighting one another, and they even shook hands.

I think both boys were relieved to avoid the fight, but they felt backed into a corner. My effort and concern for my students was so intense that for the next few days my other students would randomly say that they just saw "them" fighting just to watch me freak out and begin interrogating them about it.

For lunch, I never had lunch alone when I taught. In fact, I had more kids in my room for lunch than I did in my classes! This was the time that we could talk about things other than my assignments and I really got to know my students. Sometimes I would get some work done while I listened to their silly antics, other times I was their audience of one and was not allowed to do anything else.

One of my favorite memories is when I had just recently moved the students' desks into rows so as to be better able to monitor their devices. They really were not fond of this new arrangement, but they sat where I put them. So, on this particular day, I had to run to the restroom and told them to wait until I got back to go into my room for lunch.

I trusted these kids and was not concerned with their behavior. However, when I came back, they were seemingly out of breath and, of course, I had to demand an answer as to why this was the case. They gave me no reason, and so I was very suspicious and let them know that I wasn't pleased with their coyness. Just as I was trying my best to seem like an authority figure,

I opened my door (which I left unlocked) and saw that my teacher desk (that I soon got rid of because I realized I'd rather stand) was moved magically right in the center of the classroom, plopped down in the sea of student desks.

They began laughing proudly before I even spoke a word. I was amazed, it was like magic! I thought this to be a great little prank, and I took it not only in stride, but also as a challenge.

My revenge? I sat at my desk just as they moved it, and they were ever so upset to have a teacher sit directly among them all in class every day. After about a week I grew tired of my revenge, and they moved it back for me – happily I might add.

The Takeaway

♦ I have so many stories that I can share during times that many others spent alone in their rooms or in the faculty room. I would never tell another teacher that they should give up their lunch, but you may be surprised that even if it's only once a month that you spend lunchtime with students, it is a truly eye-opening and wholesome practice.

IV

Things They Cannot Teach You in College

25

Teacher Survival Guide

15 Things You Do Not Want to Be Without

Here are some things that you can only learn on the job when teaching. Therefore, if you are new to the profession, accept the gold that only comes with experience.

1. Clothing

Every school has its own climate. Often school buildings can resemble an ocean, as you walk through them you may encounter warm or cold areas. The most important thing is to discover the climate trends for your classroom and any other area that you may have a duty in, such as the cafeteria. In New Jersey, we have to layer clothing most of the year due to the ever-changing climate; however, this is also how you should dress for teaching. Always have the following in your classroom:

- Cardigan
- Appropriate short-sleeve shirt
- Change of socks
- A scarf
- The in-case-of-emergency change of shirt or pants

DOI: 10.4324/9781003370161-29

I have a cardigan that is neutral in color in my room at all times, I don't even take it home. I also have a lightweight shirt for the days when the air conditioner stops or the heater is set to "core Earth" temperatures. The change in socks is crucial in case your feet are cold or one sock is protesting and every two minutes you need to adjust it. Like the cardigan, the scarf never leaves my room. As for the emergency change of clothes, never think that you are above needing them – coffee spills on the commute to work, a new tear in your clothing, or a stain you didn't notice when you were half asleep dressing in the morning.

2. Snacks

Look in a teacher's desk or closet and you will always know if they are a career teacher because they have snacks. Not for the kids! Though some of us have those as well. Teaching schedules are strong suggestions, but often they do not reflect your actual daily routine. Many of us go through the entire day without having an opportunity to sit and eat lunch. Phone calls, copies, students who need your ear or your help, colleagues who talk you into a corner, class coverages, fire drills, the list goes on and on! Always have something in your room that you can eat while walking. A bag of chips, peanut butter filled pretzels, granola bars, anything that you can carry and has some protein to fuel you. Teenagers require a lot of patience, and if you are hangry (hungry-angry) you are setting yourself up to snap. I read a study years ago with data to prove that more convicts were granted parole after the parole board ate lunch. The earlier cases had a lower percentage of approval. We may not be a sentencing board in a prison, but we have the power to make a student's day horrible if we are not properly nourished.

3. Lotion

This one is for both you and the students, especially if you live in a place where winters get very cold. I often have students ask me for hand lotion in class. I always keep a nicely scented bottle on my desk. Just as important are your hands, if you are lucky enough to use the restroom during the day, or if you have to pump hand sanitizer all day long, you will need lotion. The moment you attempt to pass out papers to your class with hands that are dry, you will understand its importance.

4. Batteries

Something in your room will need batteries one day when you are least expecting it, believe me. I always have AA or AAA. Whenever that moment comes, my lesson will not be destroyed because of dead batteries.

5. Copy/Printer Paper

At least in New Jersey, we are always battling the paper budget. Many times, our entire building will be out of paper for copies. I always keep at least one ream of paper in my room, hidden from other frantic teachers who cannot make copies of their assignments.

6. Printer

It may be an expensive purchase, but it will be worth its value tenfold by the end of the year. Have you changed your plans at the last minute? You do not have to wait in the copier line and pray to get copies before the bell rings. Toner cartridge out on the copier? You still can make "copies" of your assignments. Ask your technology department to connect it to your computer, if possible with real wires, so that when the Wi-Fi is down, you can still function!

7. A Personal Hotspot

Most cell phone carriers offer this as an added feature for your cell phone. Without fail, the Internet connection in your classroom will fail. My personal hotspot has saved the day for me more than once. Also, if you are using the school computer or device for personal reasons, it's nice not to be stalked at the IP address of the school. I often use my banking application and prefer to keep it off of their server.

8. A Small Space Heater/Air Conditioner

I know what you're thinking, these things are a fire safety hazard. Yes, they are, and I respect that. Still, I respect my toes and having a small plug-in heater under my desk is sometimes the only way I can get through the day. I also will put it in front of the room for my students, the same for the AC. Students cannot learn if they are freezing or sweating, just set a reminder to turn it off between classes and at the end of the day. Also, don't tell anyone that you read this in my book.

9. Single Cup Coffee Maker

Staying with the theme of fire hazards, if you are the typical caffeine-addicted teacher, then you understand the importance of being able to make a cup of coffee during the day. Some faculty rooms have them already, and some schools even brew a big pot (these are the best schools), but you never want to be stuck without access to coffee or tea during a long day teaching. Therefore, buy some of those cardboard coffee cups, or keep a few mugs in your room with a box of creamers. I have coffee, tea, honey, water for the coffee maker, a stirring spoon, and extra creamers in my room. I cannot tell you how critical this supply is to my enthusiasm levels. If you cannot sneak a coffee maker into your room, think about starting a coffee club. Each month collect $20 from the other coffee-lovers in your school and use the money to buy coffee and creamers. Brew a pot for everyone to enjoy and access in a safe spot like the cafeteria or teacher's lounge. I was part of a coffee club at one school, and it was pure genius!

10. Plastic or Reusable Utensils

I promise that one day you will be starving and that will be the day that you forgot to pack utensils with your lunch. Until you've eaten a salad with your fingers, you won't really appreciate the function of a fork!

11. Band-Aids

Some schools supply a few bandages for teachers to have in their rooms, but I like to know I have enough. First, it stops a student from having to leave the room to go to the nurse in case of a paper cut or a hangnail. Second, I buy fun ones that are meant for little kids and it gives my students a bit of a laugh to have a dinosaur or Hello Kitty band-aid.

12. Bluetooth Speaker

A cheap version will do, but you need something to play music on from your device. I use music a lot in my lessons, even during tests I will play piano music or jazz when they are writing. Holiday music is also always welcomed in many classes. Do not rely on your computer as you may need to use it for another purpose. Having the flexibility of using your phone is great. Also, I like to use the *Jeopardy!* theme or a buzzer sound when playing review games.

13. File Folders

I name a folder for every lesson that I teach, such as "Farming Villages" or "Transitions" and I place at least one copy of the PPT, notes, or handout that we used in class. It is easy to access when a student loses a copy or is absent, and, when I am done teaching the skill, I file it and now all I have to do is pull the file the following year. My filing cabinet is full of lesson "master copies" for every skill that I have taught over the years. Sometimes I add to them or get rid of some, but I have a cabinet that I can easily walk my fingers through for every lesson I need to teach. It is important to create the folder as soon as you make class copies. It sits on my desk in a file rack until I no longer need it, then I file it. If you wait to make the folder, you'll most likely end up tossing your materials and you'll start at square one the following year. Some teachers love electronic copies of everything, but I caution you against that, technology can sabotage even the best-prepared lesson.

14. Change of Shoes

Ladies, this is mostly for you. You know how comfortable those cute new shoes can seem at 6:00 am, and then they turn into torture devices by lunch. Always keep a neutral pair of "safe" shoes in your room.

15. A Tiny Medicine Cabinet

In a locked drawer or in a purse, be sure to have medicine for headaches, indigestion, cough drops, and any other necessity, such as eye drops or allergy medication. Students get to go home sick, but teachers rarely do. Have what you need to make it through the day within reach of you – but not the students.

V

The Real Reason I Am a Teacher

26

True Stories

I Cannot Make This Stuff Up

The best part of teaching is the kids, if you're doing it right. Here are some of my favorite stories from my years of teaching.

"The Magnet"

♦ I had one male student whose locker was directly across from my door where I stood every morning before homeroom began. He was late to homeroom every day by about thirty seconds. It was just late enough to have to acknowledge it, but nothing so egregious that I decided to penalize him for it.

One morning I watched him walk around the hallway with a female student from another homeroom. As they passed me, about three minutes before the bell rang (because he was also the FIRST student to walk off the buses every morning so he got a full ten minutes before homeroom), I told him that he could be early if he came into the room now. Of course, he looked at the female student he was with and laughed me off.

When he was thirty seconds late to homeroom that morning, I had to call him out (not in front of other students) for being right outside the door two minutes ago, yet still being late. I tried to give him an ultimatum in

DOI: 10.4324/9781003370161-31

my toughest "teacher voice" that he needed to be on time from now on or he would get a late pass. In reaction to this, he quickly played the victim and blamed all his "lates" on the girls who drag him through the halls. "All the girls?" I asked. He then rambled out a list of girls and seemingly complained about how hard it was for him due to his huge female following.

My response was to feign empathy for the horrible circumstance he was in. Last class of the day I taught my homeroom students, and, as this student walked past me at the door and toward his desk, I randomly came up with his new nickname. (I stood at my door and welcomed every single student into my room before every class – even the teenagers who rolled their eyes eventually said hello by June!) I said, "Hello, magnet." Though he was used to my strange nicknames by this point in the year, he stopped and asked for an explanation. I was so proud of myself and told him, "Well, you must be a magnet because all those girls keep attaching themselves to you despite your attempts to keep them away. You're like a magnet, they cannot help themselves!"

He threw his head back and laughed. These small inside jokes were a part of my daily routine with my students; this is why they are my favorite part of the day. However, sometimes they never cease to make me laugh. The next morning things were back to routine, and I was standing by my door and this student was nowhere to be seen. I figured maybe he was driven to school and therefore late. However, just as I was about to close my door, he turned the corner. He went to his locker and stood right in front of it, oddly looking right at me. When I told him to come into the room, he said, "I can't move," and for a moment I thought he was ill until my adult brain slowly caught onto his joke. He was a magnet, so therefore he was "stuck" to his locker. This is the obvious joke; however, he went through the entire act of slowly pulling his limbs from the locker as he came into the room. He then, of course, was attracted to the metal desks on his way to his seat. I was hysterical – the class was mostly confused.

As you may guess, this nickname gave me months of entertainment as he continued to randomly get stuck against lockers down the hall when he noticed I was at my door on duty between classes. I'd just shake my head and giggle at his full commitment to this character he so happily adopted.

Random student quotes:

- ♦ "I was making my cat a salad …"
- ♦ "Mrs. Matusz, snakes can't run, right?" (this was a debate I had to settle in the hallway)
- ♦ "I wish a little terrorist threw something at me." Referring to my son (the little terrorist) giving out random classroom tickets on Bring Your Child to Work Day.

"Obituary for a Skeleton"

- ♦ I had a student who was very guarded. I didn't know much about him as it was only October, but he would seemingly be depressed some days and happy others. I believe it turned out that he had a girlfriend with whom he fought.

  One particular day I was having a fun lesson and almost every student was smiling – except this student. He was working independently, and I got an idea. I walked over to my shelf where I had a collection of knickknacks and picked up my Yankees bear stuffed animal, about the size of a coffee mug, and silently placed it on his desk as I strolled by without saying a word.

  He looked at it and looked at me, inquisitively as you may imagine. I said, "Thought you could use a friend, you look a little down." He acted like he wasn't amused, but when he paired up for work another student tried to touch it and he possessively moved it closer to him and claimed it as *his* friend. Other students asked for "friends," but I said that I didn't choose, the "friends" chose. Every day from that day forward that student came in, took the bear off my shelf, and placed it on his desk, then returned it at the end of class.

Fast forward a few weeks and all the items on my shelves were "borrowed" as desk friends in that class. A sea of 13-year-olds who were too cool for school had bears, animal erasers, plastic historical figurines, animal candles, etc. sitting on their desks as I taught about ancient societies. These are the moments teachers live for.

About five years later I remembered this and brought in some small stuffed animals for a sixth grade class I was temporarily teaching. I don't know if it was the age or the creativity level, but this took on a completely different angle.

My students "adopted" my animals and when I allowed them to take full, legal custody of them it became even more interesting. My animals had clothes, new outfits every day; later, I discovered they were borrowed from the American Doll collection. They also had their own beds and bedrooms at the students' houses!

One day, my three-year-old son came into work with me and he accidentally broke a "friend" that a student had left in the room. I figured it may be upsetting when I had to break the news to her, but my student was on the verge of tears. To help imagine this conversation, the "friend" she was attached to was a plastic skeleton of a crow from the dollar store Halloween section. If you find it strange that a 12-year-old girl would bond with a bird skeleton, then you will be very surprised to find out that, ultimately, she wrote an obituary that she had asked to read to the class. She fought back tears while reading it. True story. I replaced it with one of my son's old toys he didn't play with. She was slow to embrace HeyHey, the rooster from Moana, but eventually she accepted the "alive" plush animal. To this day, that obituary is on my "student wall of fame" that is full of memories that I take down and put up no matter where I move to.

"YOUR MOM"

♦ One year, the phrase, "Your mom," was popular for the kids to throw around to each other. Eighth grade students have a canny ability to use such phrases to make every situation slightly inappropriate. Usually, it was said quietly to another student and took on the "That's what she said," connotation.

Having taught eighth grade for years, this was hardly anything new.

Other than correcting them if I overheard it, it was just another trend that became insidious in middle school.

It was one thing to quietly whisper it to a friend, but once a very bold student took it farther than any student had.

I asked the student a question during classwork, and he made the unfortunate decision to respond with this phrase, "Your mom." Due to the question I had asked him, his response suggested that he was romantically involved with *my mother*! The entire class began to crack up laughing after a pregnant pause to see if I was going to yell at him or laugh. Of course, I couldn't help myself, I laughed.

Even though I was shocked by his audacity, it was said in jest and by no means was this student mean hearted. He looked as shocked as I was when it came out of his mouth.

I took in the situation and let the class calm down. Once it was quiet (after only a few seconds), I looked straight-faced at him and said, "(Name), my mother is 70 years old." This was perfect because it was true, and he immediately regretted his comment. The class ooed and aahed as they giggled at his red face.

We left it at that for the rest of the class. But, as I have always been one for practical jokes and I didn't appreciate his smart comment that he felt bold enough to make, I had to revisit it. I was on lunch duty at a school that had a ping pong table in the dining hall.

Toward the end of lunch, I walked over to him at his table and offered him a challenge: if he played me in ping pong and I won, then he would have to "break up" with my mom. The enthusiasm was met with his disbelief, and we played a very close game in front of the other students who were in his class. Of course, I won.

27

Proceed with Caution

When I say that the kids are the best part of the job, I mean it. They do become "your kids." But this also can take the biggest toll on your life if tragedy strikes.

One year I had a student who said very little in my classes, but she began coming to my room for lunch. She had lots of friends, but she was seemingly shy around teachers. I had her in my class and was going through my gradebook calling students up to my desk to have a "come to Jesus" talk about their grades going into the last semester. (I think it's important to note here that I didn't just talk about their grades in my class. I looked at all of their classes and asked if they were falling behind in any class and what the reason was. Sometimes this would lead us into a conversation about their potential, and the crew they gave their time to.) So, near the top of my roster, was my student named Di'jana. In my best *The Price Is Right* voice I said, "Deee-Jhanna … come on down!" No one moved. Because this student was more reserved than others, I realized I never really had to say her name in class very often.

The awkward silence was broken with her friends laughing at her, and calling her Deee-JHA-NAA They could see by the confusion on my face that I needed clarification. "It's Dee-Jha-Nay," she finally corrected. I immediately felt like a dunce. I asked her if it was true that she had allowed me to call her by the wrong name for the last eight months. It was true. This is a lesson I still

DOI: 10.4324/9781003370161-32

take with me. I always preface my first day with setting the tone that I WANT to call students by the name they were given, and please correct me if I am just making up a name by pronouncing it wrong.

It was almost like now that I knew her name, her wall was down. In those last few months her and I grew to be very close. She was always in my room, sometimes when she was supposed to be "in the bathroom." I think I bonded with her so quickly because I could appreciate the distance that she always put between herself and her emotions. I also deferred to humor instead of honest emotions in my life. Her smile was contagious and it turned out that she was also hilarious.

I remember her coming back to visit me when she went to high school. She had only been in ninth grade for about a month. She walked into my room unannounced while I was grading. She had seemed "lost" and was throwing out all kinds of "options" she was considering – none of which were healthy or smart. After hearing her speak so flippidly about her future and basically throwing it all away on a whim, I decided to do what she needed. I got tough with her.

I called her out on her "theories" and how they contradicted everything she stood for. I pointed out that she would be following the path of people whom she had talked to me about many times because she hated them for their decisions. I asked her if her goal was to become one. I remember her spinning around in my teacher chair, seeming uncomfortable with the scolding. We left off on good terms, but it was a side of me she had never seen, and something I had not shown to many of my kids. If nothing else, she got the message that I cared about her. And part of me felt like she just wanted to see if I really did.

I continued my mentorship role with her throughout the years. I watched her basketball games, I gave her advice when she called me about tough situations, and I consoled her when life reared its unforgiving head. She messaged me through Facebook on my birthday every year and often on Mother's Day.

"Happy Mother's Day, as you technically only have one child you're like the mom I never had."

One message, "Hey Mrs. Matusz could you send me your number? I would like to talk to you about something I have no one else to talk to." I am not going to reveal her personal struggles, but I remember just telling her that it would be OK and I was here.

In the midst of COVID-19, March 2021, we made plans to meet up. I kept an eye on her through Facebook and was overjoyed to see that she had found her authentic self and seemed to be so happy. She no longer had that "lost" look. She was found by someone who saw her and loved her. I messaged her when I was back in her town, but because I didn't have her phone number saved, she didn't see the message until I was already leaving. We said we'd meet up soon, and that we would "hold each other to it."

Meanwhile, she was excelling at her artwork and was actively writing and performing poetry. I watched from a distance, proud of my "kid," always commenting on her posts and encouraging her.

Then in February 2022 I received a message on Facebook from another one of her classmates who kept in touch with me. He didn't often message me privately, so when I saw it pop up on my phone during my prep, I immediately looked to read it:

"Hey have you been in contact with Di'jana or anyone she's close to?"

I replied, "Yes, she is my friend on Facebook and just responded to my post (of when I took her out to get sushi for lunch and filmed her dramatic response to eating a cucumber roll) the other day."

"Why, what's up?"

He responded, "Are you busy?"

I text, "I'm on my prep."

"I can talk"

Pretty much no matter what I am doing, if a former student reaches out to me I make myself available. Think about it, if you are a teenager or young adult reaching out to your former teacher, you probably really need them to be there for you at that moment. I was preparing for my second teaching observation that morning. My prep is first period, and my principal was coming to observe me for the first time, in a new district, during my third period class. Thus, fellow educators can understand that I was a bit distracted.

The next message was a link to an article:

Woman, 19, killed in head-on NJ crash Police Say

Then my former kid messaged, "I'm not 100% I haven't talked to anyone yet but I don't know who to contact."

My response, "Fuck. OK."

Now, this kid was 19, out of HS, and I just wrote what I was thinking. My exact thoughts, "fuck … OK." It was me talking to myself. OK … OK … it's gonna be OK. Now what? OK."

He then went on to say that he was sorry for telling me at work but he didn't know anyone else with her name and that he knew how close we were.

How close we "were."

At this point I had read the short article and I knew it was her. Her first and last names were unique, and it happened not far from where I taught her in the same county.

My response, "It has to be her. What the Fuck-19."

So what do moms do when their kid passes away too early? I cannot imagine losing my biological kid, but this hit very close to my heart.

I reached out to her sister who I found through Facebook and asked for service details and offered to buy her casket spray. One of the hardest things was to pick out the flowers that I would bury with her. I picked out the most beautiful ones I could find to be placed on top of, and inside, the casket. Selfishly, I wanted to have a piece of me, or something I gave her, to be buried with her – not just tossed in the garbage.

But it wasn't enough. I couldn't let her be another young kid taken from the world without expressing how special she was to me. I asked to read something at her funeral.

I am not a poet, but I knew she was very poetic later in her life. So I wrote a poem to her, and I read it to her closed casket and her family in the pews. All the while, I could hear her voice in my mind making fun of me.

I still hear her whenever I take life too seriously. For example, when I finally did get observed by my principal two class periods after I learned that she had passed. I was in an emotionally raw place, and I did not disclose it to my principal. While trying to stay steady and focused on my lesson in front of the room, my co-teacher and I looked at each other because my voice was some-how coming through my TV smartboard, like radio feedback.

We tried trouble-shooting it, and she and I stopped the lesson to try to fix it. We both had never experienced this before. It got to the point where I could no longer delay my observation, and so every time I wanted to address my class, I was forced to walk to the back of the classroom, far away from the screen, and anytime I forgot it'd ring out in my echo and I'd be reminded to stand at the back of the room.

I was overwhelmed by the day already, when I looked over at my principal who sat at my desk taking notes and I noticed she was laughing. "I think it's funny," she said.

Then it hit me; and I mumbled on my walk over to the corner, "Fucking Di'jana." I smiled and felt my eyes water up. As if that wasn't enough, for the rest of the lesson and the year, my "pen" color would randomly change mid-sentence while writing on my board. Sometimes it would change to the "eraser" mode and actually erase what I was trying to highlight or underline.

Whether or not her energy was with me that day, I somehow *knew* she was OK, still being her wise-ass self, just in another realm.

So, as I say, once my kid, always my kid.

The eulogy I read for Di'jana at her service:

Dii j… to me you were DijanaE – though you let me call you DiJANNa for the first month of school.

When we first met you had little to say
You were quiet, kept to yourself
But your smile began to show a little bit more each day
Your sincerity and authenticity set you apart from others
That's why there's so many of us here today struggling to recover—
From a loss
That seems insurmountable
Because you were so damn relatable
In the short span of only 19 years on this Earth
You - Created art

- *Spoke your truth to power*
- *And never let others forget their worth*

- *Philosophical*
- *Inquisitive*
- *and proud*

Once a quiet 8th grader …
… Became a woman who lived out loud
The energy you exuded
Was the kind, that made everyone around you feel included
Maybe at times, it was yourself that you searched for
You'd ask the big questions, <u>knowing</u> there was so much more—-
… To this thing … called Life
That you have left without warning
Now a star adorning
The moon at night
I know that your energy remains here, but it still just doesn't seem right
A young person whose soul was always glowing
Making people happier without even knowing

And yet –
Here you lie
And I keep wondering <u>WHY?</u>
Diij, I promise to keep you alive through your stories
You have left us all with so many memories of you dancing and making jokes
We have plenty of material, so you don't have to worry
In fact, I imagine that you danced yourself into whatever realm comes next
I can see you now with that swag and those outfits earning you respect
But …
while you are partying above …
Don't forget about the ones down here that you loved
Please remind us not to take life so seriously once in awhile
… And Diij,
if you have the power to
Please let us never forget your smile.